Build Your Own Home Network

Ron Gilster and
Diane McMichael Gilster

Build Your Own Home Network

MCGRAW-HILL
Professional Book Division

New York / St. Louis / San Francisco / Auckland / Bogotá / Caracas
Lisbon / London / Madrid Mexico City / Milan / Montreal / New Delhi
San Juan / Singapore / Sydney / Tokyo / Toronto

McGraw-Hill

A Division of The McGraw-Hill Companies

2 3 4 5 6 7 8 9 0   QPD/QPD   0 5 4 3 2 1 0

ISBN 0-07-212466-0

The sponsoring editor for this book was Michael Sprague and the production manager was Clare Stanley. It was set in Melior by Patricia Wallenburg.

Printed and bound by Phoenix Book Technology.

c o n t e n t s

Our objective in writing this book was two-fold. First of all, we wanted to educate you on the concepts and practices of networking computers in general. Secondly, we wished to provide a no-frills, step-by-step guideline that somebody with only basic computer skills could use to create a home computer network.

We have tried very hard to create a simple, step-by-step, descriptive guideline that you can follow to create your own home network without making all of the mistakes usually necessary to gain this knowledge. We explain the terms and concepts of networking, in general, and how each networking component is used and why. We hope that armed with a basic understanding of the language of networking, you will be able to hold your own against the jargon-tongued super-geeks you may encounter at the computer supply stores. If you want an in-depth explanation of networking, its components, and all of its applications, this isn't the book for you. However, if you are looking for a book to help you to install a network in your home (or business), you've found it!

There are many reasons why you should want to network your home computers. Chief among the reasons is that it allows you to share all of those really expensive peripherals and services. Without a network, you must either have two of everything—printers, modems, scanners, Internet connections, and more—or take turns using these resources. Among other reasons to network your home computers are that you can share data and play those really nifty network games with other family members, saving the cost of those trips to the video arcade at the mall.

In providing you with the steps used to create a network and a list of the parts and components you need to do so, we have avoided quoting any prices or brands, except when it was unavoidable. This is primarily because computer component prices fluctuate almost daily and brands come and go or are more or less available due to their popularity. A certain brand of network interface card that may have been very popular at the time we are writing this book, may be very expensive or hard to find due to demand when you are reading this. We aren't trying to create snob networks with all of the "right" parts; we just want to help you to create the best and most functional network possible. There are many interchange-able brands of components, so this is best left neutral. Please don't misun-derstand any brands shown in our illustrations as an endorsement of that particular brand. However, one brand we couldn't avoid was Microsoft Windows, for hopefully obviously reasons.

Installing a home network doesn't need to require ten years of experience and an engineering degree. It is really a simple matter of assembling the right parts, installing them in the right places, and configuring the right software so that they all talk with each other. Sound simple? Well, it is!

We hope you learn a little and gain a home network as a result of this book.

CHAPTER 1

Network Basics

Before you begin building your own home network, there are a few basics we think you should review first. The fact that you purchased, or are thinking of purchasing, this book indicates that you think you could use just a little bit of help in this endeavor. If you review the terminology and concepts in this chapter, then at least you will be able to "talk the talk," a very important skill as you venture out to buy the components for your network, and, later to impress your friends. With the parts in hand, by following the step-by-step process detailed in the chapters that follow, you will be able to complete the installation of your network.

This chapter is divided into three sections. The first section defines some of the commonly used terminology of networks, which provides you with a grounding in the terms that you need to know to identify, compare, install, and operate your network. The second section of this chapter includes an overview of general networking concepts. The third section provides a quick look at bandwidth and how the different networking elements can have an impact on it.

The mission of this book is to help you install the first two work-stations of your own home network. The assumption is that you have had little or no experience with this sort of thing and need a detailed step-by-step procedure that you can follow to successfully install your first network. Should you need it, there is also a glossary of commonly used networking terms and concepts included in the back of this book. However, anywhere we use a new term or reference a networking concept for the first time, we will provide you with at least a quick definition or example. It is our hope that you come away from this experience with not only a fully functioning home network but also with some good networking knowledge.

Common Networking Terminology

Before you walk into the local computer superstore to buy the components you need to build your own home network, you should review for understanding some commonly used networking terms. Those 18-year-olds at the computer store have no problem using every computer and networking term they know or have ever heard of, to impress, and possibly intimidate you. To win this war of words, you have two choices: learn the language or order online. Actually, you have only one choice—learn the language—because even ordering online requires that you know and understand the specification of a networking component.

This section provides you with some of the very basic terms and concepts, so that even if you can't speak networking fluently, you will be able to at least understand it, provided it's spoken slowly enough.

What is a Computer Network?

Essentially, a *computer network* is two or more computers or peripheral devices, such as printers, CD-ROM towers, scanners, and the like, that are directly connected for the purpose of sharing the hardware, software, and data resources of the connected devices. Figure 1.1 illustrates a network in its most basic form: two computers directly connected with a cable. Depending on the configuration of the computers, each computer user can share data and devices on his or her computer with the user at the other computer and access data and devices stored on and attached to the other computer. We'll discuss how this is done in Chapter 4.

Figure 1.1

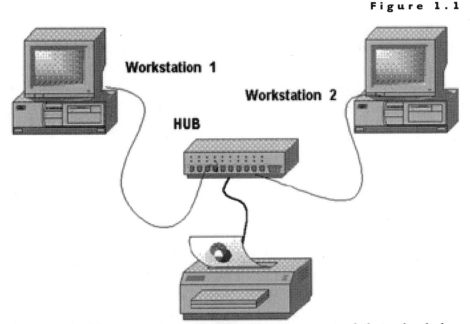

A network with two computers and a printer connected through a hub.

As shown in Figure 1.1, a network consists of three fundamental parts:

- Devices to be connected, such as computers, printers, hubs, etc.

- The wires, cables, or other media used to connect the network's devices.

- The network adapters used to connect the cables to the computer (because the network adapter is generally installed inside the computer's case, it is not visible in this drawing)

Networks can be created in many shapes and sizes, but most home networks are simple affairs much like that shown in Figure 1.1. Two, or perhaps more, computers are connected to one another with a standard cable attached to network adapters installed inside of or attached to each computer.

Workstations and Nodes

When you add a computer into a network, it becomes a workstation or a node. A *workstation* is a computer that has been attached to the network. Workstation is just another way to say "networked computer." A *node* is how the network sees the workstation or any other device that has been attached to the network. A node, a term derived from the word *nodule*, is actually the reference point used by the network to identify anything attached to the network.

In effect, the network knows a workstation as a node much like the postal service knows your house by its location and street address. To the network, the location (address) of a workstation is synonymous with its node identity, so the term *node* is used interchangeably with the term *workstation*. In other words, a workstation can also be called a node, and vice versa.

Network Adapters

Chapter 2 provides a deeper look at the other parts of the network, including the cabling or connecting media and the network adapter, but here is a quick overview of these two essential parts of the network. They are essential because without them you are left with *stand-alone* computers, which cannot share resources except over a sneaker-net. A *sneaker-net* is a set of computers that share data only through a person physically carrying a diskette or other storage medium from one machine to another.

The network adapter allows a workstation to communicate with the other network elements. It receives and translates incoming signals from the network for the workstation and translates and sends outgoing communications to the network. A network interface card, NIC; see Figure 1.2), is the most common type of network adapter, and is generally installed inside the computer's case in an expansion slot located on the computer's main board. NIC is pronounced just like the name "Nick."

We should point out that not all network adapters are NICs, which means some network adapters, as we will discuss in Chapter 2, are not installed inside of the computer. However, the NIC is by far the most common form of network adapter used to connect home and office computers to a network.

Network Cabling and Media

The most commonly used type of network cable is an unshielded twisted pair (UTP). UTP, illustrated in Figure 1.3, is unshielded copper wire in which insulated strands of copper wire are twisted in pairs over each other. This type of cabling is easily found and generally inexpensive.

Don't misunderstand the use of the word *unshielded* in UTP. What this means is that the entire cable is not shielded from outside interference from other wires or electrical noise sources. The plastic insulation on each wire does not provide a great deal of protection from electrical interference. The plastic sheath that covers the entire cable bundle is not considered an electrical shield. We also discuss some of the properties and limitations of UTP and other wire types later in this chapter.

Figure 1.2

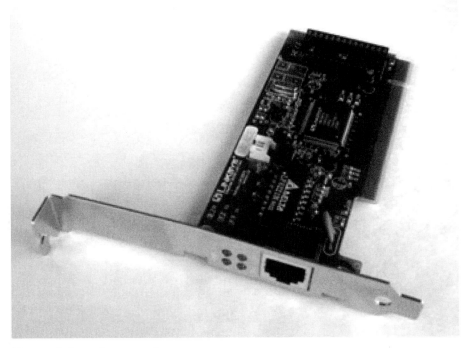

Network interface card.

Figure 1.3

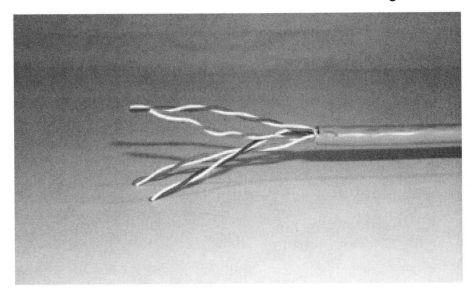

Unshielded twisted pair (UTP) wire.

There are several other types of cables that can be used to connect a network, including coaxial cable, shielded twisted pair (STP), fiber optic, and even the existing telephone or electrical power lines in the walls of your home. The other types of cabling used in computer networks are:

- **Coaxial cabling:** This cable, illustrated in Figure 1.4, is very much like that used to connect your television set to the cable box and the VCR. There are actually two types of coaxial cable used in networks, a thick wire and a thin wire. See Chapter 2 for more information on coaxial cables.

Figure 1.4

A sample of thin coaxial cabling.

- **STP:** This is a version of twisted copper wiring in which the bundle of twisted copper wires in the cable is shielded with a metal sheath that absorbs electromechanical interference (EMI), which can come from other cables, light fixtures, and other electrical devices and wires by which the cable passes. STP is more expensive and, more than what's required for most home networks. Figure 1.5 shows the layer of an STP cable.

- **Fiber optic:** This type of cabling technology uses thin strands of glass, as shown in Figure 1.6, to carry digital data that has been transformed into light impulses. It is very expensive, hard to work with, and certainly not worth the effort for a home network. We won't be spending much time on fiber optic cabling in this book. You'll need to wait for the sequel, "How to Build Your Own Corporate Network Backbone," for that discussion.

Figure 1.5

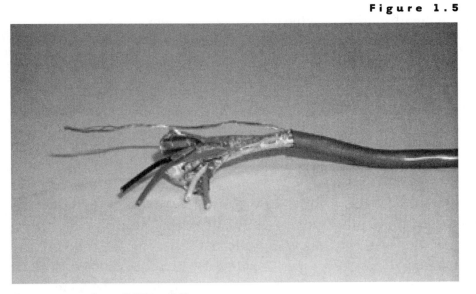

A cross-section of STP cabling.

Figure 1.6

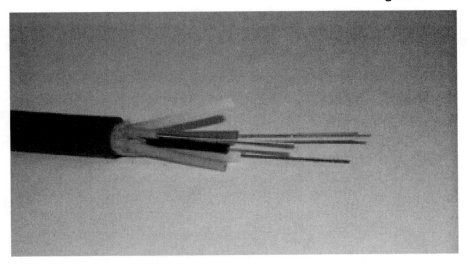

A piece of fiber optic cabling.

■ **Existing wiring:** There are newly released network media technologies that allow you to build your network, using special network adapters, over the existing telephone and power lines in the walls of your home. This will be discussed more fully in Chapter 2 in the discussion on home networking kits.

Media refers to the material and make up of the cable used in your network. If you use UTP, then unshielded twisted pair copper is the network medium of your network. *Medium* is the singular form and *media* is the plural form. Because most networks have only one cable type, they are said to have a *single connection medium*. When you consider all of the various types of cabling that can be used on a network, you are talking about network media. Don't be surprised if you find that most people simply refer to the network medium as the cable or wire type.

Plug-and-Play Devices

One term that you should know before you begin choosing the components to build your network is plug-and-play. Often abbreviated by manufacturers as PnP, *plug-and-play* means that little or no manual configuration or set-up is required for the device on most computers. Plug-and-play devices are discovered by the system when they are installed. They are assigned the system resources they require to operate properly and are then enabled for use. Even though there may still be some minor set-up tasks to be done to finish the installation of a NIC, this is a handy feature for a NIC to have.

Network Classifications and Types

This section includes some additional background information that you should know before attempting your first network. If you follow the instructions in Chapters 3 and 4 of this book, you can install a home network without knowing or understanding the contents of this section, but the experience will be much better if you do.

There are many different types, arrangements, and architectures of networks, and there are just as many reasons to install one. Whatever your reason for installing a home network, you want to choose the network most appropriate for your specific application. The physical arrangement of the network, which is called its *topology* (more on this later in this chapter), can control, and be controlled by several factors, such as the network operating system, the operating system of the workstations, the type of network media, and the distance between the workstations. Figure 1.7 shows computers arranged on the *bus topology*.

Figure 1.7

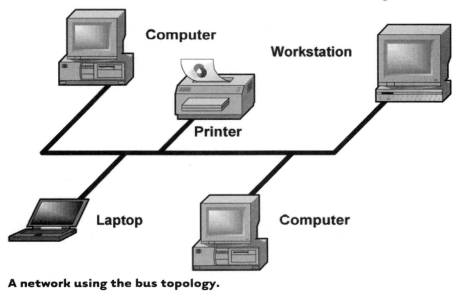

A network using the bus topology.

Network Classifications

The term *network* can be used to mean a wide range of possibilities. There are several types of network applications, each appropriate to certain networking requirements. A network, in its most basic form, is two computers connected together to share resources. The Internet, which is the global interconnection of millions of computers, is also a network. Actually, the Internet is a network of networks, but a network nonetheless. Most computer networks are somewhere between these two extremes.

Networks are grouped into several classifications or types. Below are two of the most common network classifications:

■ **Local area network (LAN):** A LAN consists of two or more nodes, usually in a relatively small (local) area. The workstations of a LAN are connected for the primary purpose of sharing local data and resources. A home network is typically a LAN, as is the network in a small office, or the one in a manufacturing plant.

■ **Wide area network (WAN):** As its name suggests, and as Figure 1.8 shows, a WAN covers a much larger area than a LAN. In fact, a WAN usually connects two or more LANs together using some form of telecommunication line, such as telephone lines or dedicated, leased high-speed lines. The network that connects the east coast office LAN with the west coast office LAN over a leased telephone line is a WAN. For future reference, the Internet is a WAN.

Figure 1.8

A Wide Area Network (WAN).

Unless you plan to go way beyond the scope of this book, your home network will be a LAN. There are emerging terms, such as SOHO (small office/home office), HPAN (home or private area network), and HAN (home area network), for the private networks installed in a home or home office, but these are merely variations of a LAN. You may see these terms when you are shopping for the components of your network.

Network Types

There are also different types of LANs. The network's type is defined by its size, its general construction, and the scope and number of resources available to its nodes. The two basic types of networks are:

- **Peer-to-peer networks:** Another name for a workstation or a node that is directly connected to another computer is a *peer*, which means that it is an equal participant in a network. Peer-to-peer networks are owned and operated cooperatively by the owners (users) of the networked workstations. Each user must decide which other users can have access to his or her computer and its resources, often on an individual basis. Most home networks are peer-to-peer networks, one of which is illustrated in Figure 1.9.

- **Client/server networks:** The other general type of network includes a computer, or *server*, that provides certain services to the other nodes, or *clients*, on the network. The server facilitates the sharing of network data, software, and hardware resources, and permission to access the resources of the network is usually managed by a single network administrator. The clients request services, such as printing a document on a network printer, access to a certain file, or to run a program, of the server and the server provides the service, data, or request. Client/server networks, like the one shown in Figure 1.10, are very common in offices with more than ten workstations and larger applications.

Figure 1.9

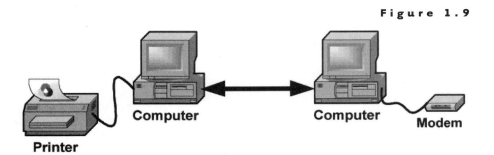

A peer-to-peer network.

Figure 1.10

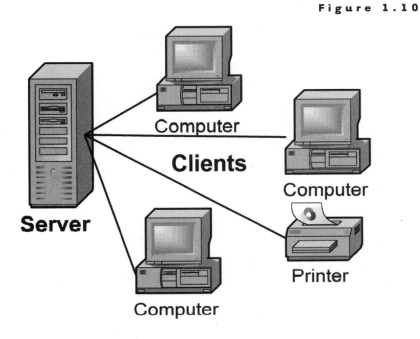

A client/server network.

Peer-to-peer networks do not include a designated server, because each peer workstation is both a server and a client. Depending on the requests being sent to it from the other peer workstations, a computer in a peer-to-peer network can be a peer, a server, or both at any given moment. This is the kind of network you will learn to build in Chapter 3.

Network Functions

Just as you don't need to be an automotive engineer to drive a car, you don't need to be a network engineer to build and use a home network. However, there are some functions of the network that you should understand, so that you can troubleshoot or upgrade your network when, or if, the time comes.

Network Protocols

Networks operate under sets of rules that prescribe how the requests, messages, and other signals are formatted and transmitted over the network. As long as all workstations are using the same set of rules to communicate over the network, the network works. However, if one workstation tries to use a different set of rules, the network will not work.

You probably follow a communications protocol of a sort everyday and perhaps aren't even aware that you do. Think about what happens in your typical telephone conversation. First you dial the number, the phone rings, and perhaps the other party answers. When they answer the phone, they say hello and you reply hello and your conversation begins. All of the variations of this process pretty much follow this same pattern, and the general pattern is the human telephonic protocol, or HTP. Actually, I made up the HTP part, but you get the idea that, when interactions between people or computers follow a standard set of rules, the results are usually higher quality communications.

The rules that govern how a network communicates are collectively called a *protocol*. There are many different protocols that are used on a network to perform different types of actions. The protocols you may encounter in building your home network are:

- **Transmission control protocol/Internet protocol (TCP/IP):** This is probably the most common protocol in use on networks today. Originally developed as the standard protocol of the Internet, it has been adapted for use on internal networks. TCP/IP is actually a suite of protocols, such as TCP, file transport protocol (FTP), point-to-point protocol (PPP), post office protocol (POP), and others, each of which set the rules and standards for a specific network action.

- **Network basic input/output system (NetBIOS):** NetBIOS is a standard network protocol that is used to support other network protocols. NetBIOS lets two computers create a connection, pass messages, and handle error detection and recovery.

- **NetBIOS extended user interface (NetBEUI):** NetBEUI adds a standard message transport option to NetBIOS. It is a very popular choice for communicating within a single LAN. NetBEUI (pronounced "net-boo-ee") will not send messages beyond the local network. Where an interface to an external network is required, such as with the Internet, NetBEUI must be adapted to another protocol, such as TCP/IP. For the home network described in this book, you will be using TCP/IP as your network protocol.

Connection Types

When computers connect with each other, whether it is over a modem or over the network, they can connect in one of two ways: connection-oriented or connection-less.

A *connection-oriented* session is the type of connection used by two modems and many networking protocols. During the noisy part of the connecting action, where the phone number of the other modem is dialed and the two modems exchange data so that they can match up and begin communicating, a connection called a *handshake* is established. From that point on, every bit of the data is managed under a connection-oriented process that acknowledges that data is received, alerts the other end when data is not received, and requests data to be retransmitted, if needed. Figure 1.11 illustrates the sequence of events in a connection-oriented dialog. Data transmitted in this type of communications session is usually organized into a bundle, called a *datagram* or *packet*. This type of connection is very reliable, but the management processes do slow things down just a bit.

The other type of connection is *connection-less*, which means that none of the handshaking and monitoring used in the connection-oriented type is going on. A connection-less session only verifies that the other end is there and then begins sending data in a stream from one point to another. Figure 1.12 contrasts how much simpler, and less reliable, a connection-less session is than the connection-oriented session shown in Figure 1.11. On your home network, you will be using a combination of connection-oriented and connection-less protocols.

Figure 1.11

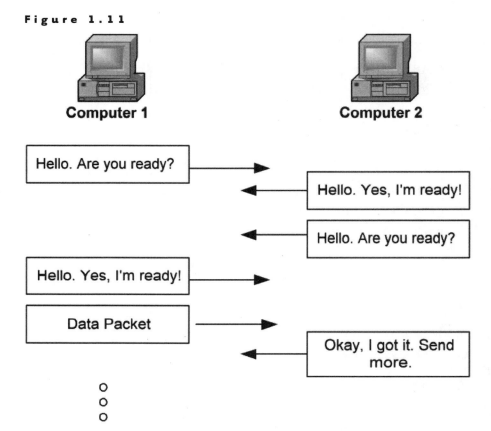

The sequence of events in a connection-oriented session.

Figure 1.12

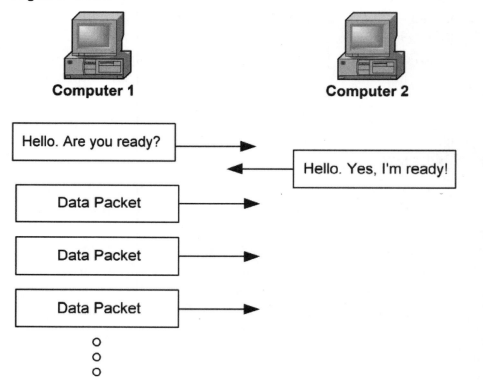

A connectionless session.

Datagrams and Packets

It isn't all that important that you know how data moves around in your network, but a little more background information can't hurt you. Network protocols organize the messages sent over the network into formatted bundles called by various names, such as datagrams, frames, and packets. Each of these terms describes a specific type of data or message bundle that is transmitted over the network for different types and levels of activity.

A *datagram*, also called a *packet*, is a small variable-length bundle of data that is usually between 256 and 2000 bytes long. A datagram is much like a letter you would send through the postal service. It contains the identity of its sender, called its *source*, the network address of its destination, and the message itself, called the *payload* in network speak. Each datagram is completely self-contained and bears no relationship to any datagram that may come after it or that came before it.

The OSI Model

You may also run into references to something called the OSI model as you study networks or read up on various products. The OSI model, which is officially the open system interconnection reference model, is a standard that defines the various functions, defined as layers, that a network packet passes through in moving from its source to its destination. The model applies to local networks and to large networks, including the Internet.

The OSI model is made up of seven layers, as shown in Figure 1.13, each of which defines an essential function that must take place to ensure that a data packet will arrive correctly at its destination. Here are the layers of the OSI model, for your information:

- **Layer 1, the physical layer,** defines how the electrical bit stream is carried over the hardware and mechanical devices of the network.

- **Layer 2, the data link layer,** supports the physical layer by providing physical device addressing, error control, and timing.

- **Layer 3, the network layer,** sends data to the part of the network on which the destination address is located. This action is called *routing* and *forwarding*.

- **Layer 4, the transport layer,** takes care of the end-to-end control of transferring data over the network.

- **Layer 5, the session layer,** sets up and terminates conversations, exchanges, and dialogs between applications over the network.

- **Layer 6, the presentation layer,** converts incoming and outgoing data from one presentation format to another. For example, the presentation layer, which is usually part of an operating system, converts a text stream into a window for display.

- **Layer 7, the application layer,** is where user authentication and privacy are considered, and constraints on data are identified.

Figure 1.13

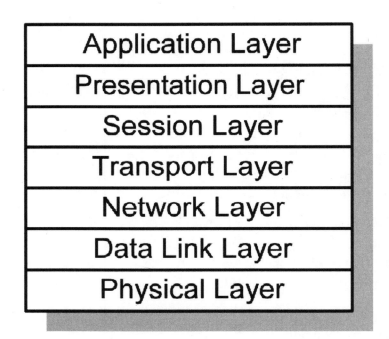

OSI Reference Model

The layers of the OSI Reference Model.

For the purposes of your home network, only the first two layers, the physical and the data link of the OSI model are important. The physical layer encompasses the wiring and connections that transmit, carry, and receive the electrical impulses representing the data sent over the network. The data link layer provides formatting, error checking, and basic addressing schemes.

Network Addressing

There are two types of addresses, MAC and IP, used on networks to send messages to their destinations as efficiently as possible. Figure 1.14 illustrates the relationship of the MAC address to the IP address on network nodes.

■ A media access control (MAC) address is the actual physical address of a node. It should not be confused with anything specific to an Apple Macintosh computer. That's a Mac and this is a MAC. The unique MAC address is permanently, electronically "burned" into network adapters, including NICs, by their manufacturer. The MAC address is used to uniquely identify each node attached to the network.

■ The Internet protocol (IP) address is made up of four 8-bit numbers (each called an *octet*) that combine to identify not only the workstation or node but also its network. We won't go into IP addressing too deeply here because there are entire books written on the classes, subnet masks, and uses of IP addresses. For our purposes, the IP address is an address that can be used to identify a workstation to the LAN, the WAN, and beyond. Every Internet host has an assigned IP address that allows other Internet hosts to access it.

Figure 1.14

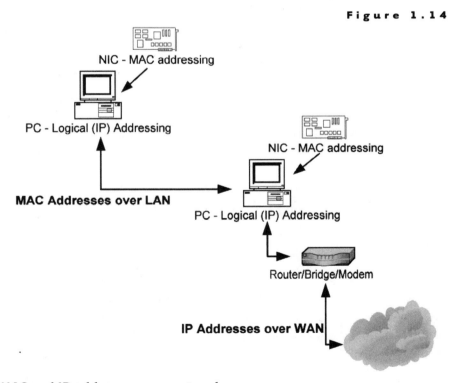

MAC and IP addresses on a network.

On the computer, there are a number of translating protocols that can be used to convert the IP address to its associated MAC address. The methods most commonly used are the TCP/IP domain name system (DNS) and the Windows Internet naming service (WINS) on Windows computers. You will see both of these again in Chapter 3 when you configure your Windows computer.

Network Topologies

Networks are often created in a general shape to accommodate the physical area into which they are installed or the technology to be used to create them. The shape and pattern used to connect the workstations to the network is its *topology*.

Here are the most common network topologies:

- **Bus:** The network nodes are connected through connectivity devices, such as a hub (more on this later in the chapter) to a central cable, called a *backbone*, that runs the length of the network. The most common networking technology, Ethernet, is installed on the bus topology. Figure 1.7 shows a bus network. We'll cover the Ethernet and the other networking technologies later in this chapter.

- **Star:** Each star network workstation is connected directly to a clustering network device, such as a hub, or even directly to the central server, creating a star-like pattern. Figure 1.15 shows a simple star network.

- **Ring:** The primary network cable is installed as a loop, or ring, and the workstations are attached to the primary cable at various points on the ring. Figure 1.16 illustrates a ring network.

- **Mesh:** Each node is connected directly to all other nodes, creating a mesh of network connections. If you want to see the layout of a mesh topology, draw four or five small circles randomly on a sheet of paper. Now connect every circle, representing a network node, to every other circle on the paper. When you are done, you will have a mess, we mean, mesh topology sample.

On your home network, you will be installing an Ethernet network on a bus topology (although with a very abbreviated backbone). You may decide to install a star topology, illustrated in Figure 1.17, on top of the bus structure using a hub, although this is necessary only if you have more than two nodes or later wish to add more devices to your network.

Figure 1.15

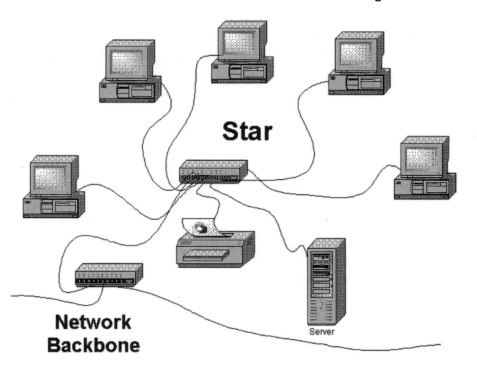

A network in a star topology.

Figure 1.16

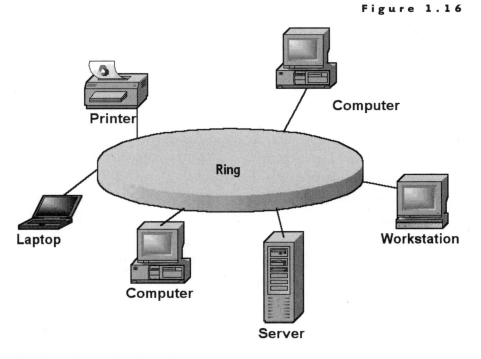

A network on a ring topology.

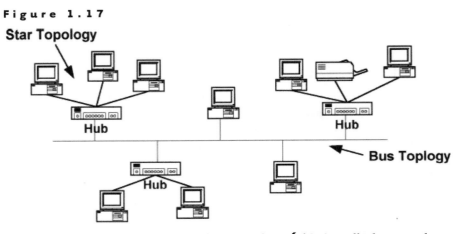

Figure 1.17

The star topology used with the bus topology (this is called a star-bus topology).

Network Technologies

This is where things can become just a little bit confusing. So far, we have discussed network protocols, network types, the OSI model, and network topologies, so what is a network technology? A network technology, which is also called a network *access method*, brings together all of the other elements to define how the network is built, how data flows over the network, and how nodes interface with the network.

The access method can be confused with the network protocol or its topology, but they are separate elements of the same network. The most popular access methods are:

- **Ethernet:** This is by far the most widely used LAN access method. It is a shared technology, which means that all workstations on the network share the available bandwidth. This means that the workstations on an Ethernet network all more or less equally split up the bandwidth available, which ranges from the standard Ethernet (called simply Ethernet or 10BaseT) of 10 million bits per second (Mbps) (Ethernet), fast Ethernet at 100 Mbps, or gigabit Ethernet at 1 Gbps (one billion bits per second). Standard Ethernet is the most commonly used access method for home networks.

- **Token ring:** This access method is the next most popular access method. It is implemented on the ring topology.

- **ARCNet:** Although its popularity is waning, there are still a few ARCNet networks around. This access method is implemented on top of the star topology.

Your home network will most likely be an Ethernet network built on a starred-bus topology to create a peer-to-peer environment. We will take another look at Ethernet networks later in this chapter when we discuss bandwidth.

Connectivity Devices

On occasion, other devices are used to provide flexibility or extended capability to the network's physical properties. Network connectivity devices are added to a network to improve its performance or extend its capabilities beyond the limitations of the media or hardware. There are a wide variety of connectivity devices on the market. For the network you will build with this book, you may need to use a hub but not any of the other connectivity devices. However, you should know the general function of the most common devices, so that you can avoid being talked into buying one.

Repeaters

A repeater is a hardware device that regenerates any signal it receives and sends it on. Just about every type of cable and wire has a distance limit after which any signal sent through it must have reached its destination or be regenerated. This is especially true with copper wire. As we will discuss later in this chapter, each different type of copper wire has a distance point at which the signal begins to fail, or *attenuate*.

Hubs

As illustrated in Figure 1.17, a hub is a network device used to connect one or more workstations to a network. This is how the hub works: the hub receives a signal from one of the devices attached to it and passes the signal on to all of its ports. The device attached to each port must decide if the forwarded signal is meant for it and, if so, act on it. For example, if a four-port hub receives a signal on its port 4, it immediately sends the message to ports 1, 2, and 3.

There are three types of hubs:

■ An **active hub** acts like a repeater to amplify the signal being passed on and like a traffic cop to avoid signal collisions. Although this sounds great, this may be more than necessary for a home network because of its cost.

- A **passive hub** does not amplify transmission signals, it merely passes along whatever it receives. This is the most common type of hub used in home networks.

- A **hybrid hub** is a hub that can mix media types (thin coaxial, thick coaxial, and UTP) and also serve as an interconnect for other hubs. It is doubtful you would have need for this type of hub in a home network, but then that really depends on the home and the network.

Routers

Just for information purposes, a router directs, or routes, packets across networks. A router works with a message's IP address to determine the best path to its destination.

Gateways

A gateway, which is usually a combination of hardware and software, is used to connect two networks with different network protocols and allow them to communicate with one another. Where a gateway will come into play on your home network is when you must designate the default gateway for your Internet services.

Network Interface Card

Every computer and peripheral device that you wish to include directly on your home network must have a NIC or network adapter, installed to connect to the network. The NIC physically connects the workstation to the network cable media and logically connects the node to the network itself. Figure 1.18 shows a common Ethernet NIC. The primary purpose of the NIC is to transmit and receive signals to and from NICs installed in other network devices. In this book, we guide you through the creation of an Ethernet network using standard NIC cards and UTP cable.

Here is a summary of the NIC and network adapter characteristics you should know:

- Each NIC is physically encoded with a unique MAC address that identifies the NIC to the network.

- A NIC is configured to the computer with a set of prescribed system resources, such as an Interrupt request (IRQ), and an input/output (I/O) address. These are the facilities used by the computer and the NIC to communicate with each other. A NIC is commonly assigned IRQ3, IRQ5, or IRQ10, and an I/O address of 300 h (h = hexadecimal) by the system (plug-and-play) or its installation software. Figure 1.19 shows a screen capture of the system resources from a Windows system. We will explain these settings in more detail in Chapters 3 and 4.

Figure 1.18

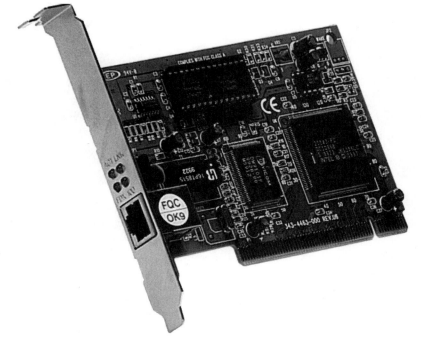

A network interface card.

- Some NICs will support more than one media type, such as UTP and coaxial, at the same time.

- Each internal NIC is designed to be compatible with a particular data bus (expansion card interface) architecture, such as peripheral component interconnect (PCI), industry standard architecture (ISA), or extended ISA (EISA).

If you plan to install a NIC in an expansion slot on your computer's motherboard, you must know the type or types of expansion slots available. If you there is only one slot available, the job is much easier, but if you have a choice, there are differences, in terms of availability, price, and capability, between the NICs designed for the different bus structures.

Figure 1.19

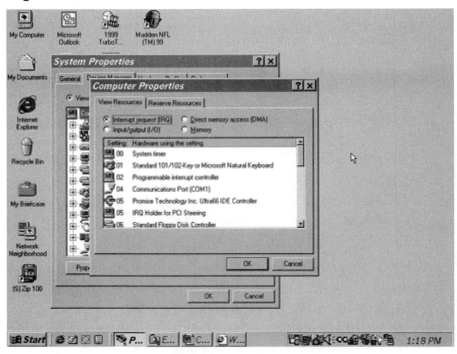

The Windows system resources dialog box.

For example, an ISA card, like the one shown in Figure 1.20, is a little less expensive, but may be harder to find. However, if you only have an EISA slot, an ISA card will work in that slot. An EISA NIC will definitely be harder to find. You may need to contact the manufacturer of your computer to find this type of NIC to fit your system. A PCI card, like the one shown in Figure 1.18, is the most commonly used type of card on newer systems and will be easy to find and buy.

Figure 1.20

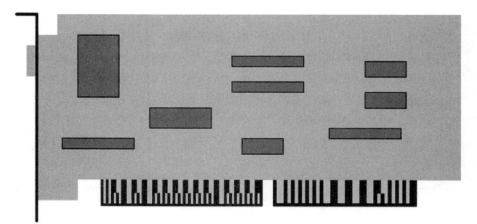

An ISA network interface card.

Getting on the Bus

Network adapters must connect two ways at once to work properly: through the network cable media and the expansion slot in the computer. Here is some general information on the bus structures commonly used for computer expansion slots:

■ ISA is an older 16-bit architecture that is still very commonly used.

■ EISA is a 32-bit architecture developed to enhance the ISA structure. ISA cards can be used in EISA slots.

■ PCI is a 32-bit architecture that is a local bus architecture, which means it shares a pathway between the CPU, memory, and peripheral devices on the computer motherboard.

■ The Personal Computer Memory Card Industry Association (PCMCIA) architecture is also called the PC card bus. It is used on notebook and other portable computers. Figure 1.21 shows a PC card NIC.

Figure 1.21

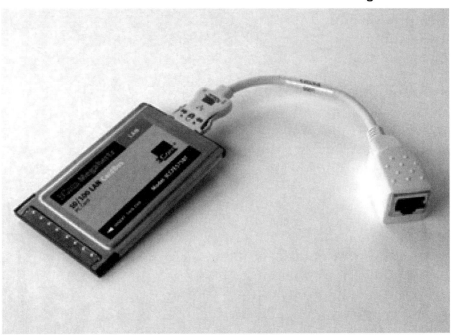

PCMCIA network adapter.

■ The universal serial bus (USB) is a plug-and-play interface that allows devices to be added to the computer without an adapter card and while it is running.

External Network Adapters

There is a variety of newer external network adapters that connect to your computer through its parallel, serial, or USB port. Figure 1.22 shows a network adapter connecting to the USB port of a notebook computer. Other types of external network adapters connect your network to your home's telephone or electrical power lines.

Figure 1.22

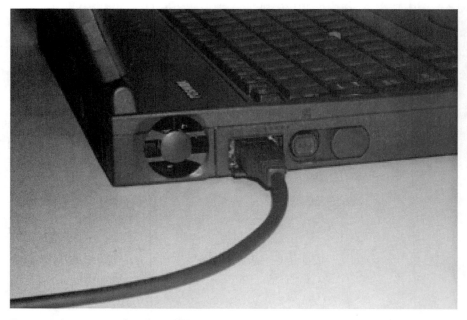

Connecting a notebook's USB port.

If you plan to use external network adapters for your home network, you can skim through most of Chapter 3, or skip it altogether. The trick to attaching an external network adapter to your computer is finding and using the correct port. Figures 1.23, 1.24, and 1.25 show the location of these ports on most desktop, tower, and portable computers, respectively.

Transceiver Types

Most NICs have their transceiver (the device that transmits and receives data to and from the network) on the adapter card itself. There are other types of NICs, in particular coaxial cable network adapters, that use an external transceiver. External transceivers attach to the network adapter in the computer through what is called a *patch cord*, which has a special type of connector, an adapter unit interface (AUI), on it. The external transceiver is attached to the network backbone with a *piercing tap* that is also called a *vampire tap*. This arrangement is illustrated in Figure 1.26.

Figure 1.23

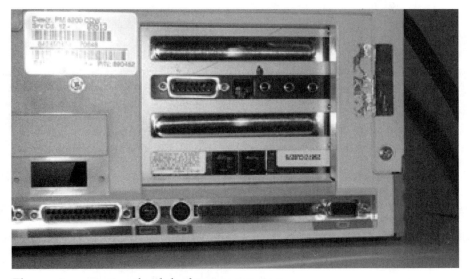

The ports on a standard desktop computer.

Figure 1.24

The ports on a tower personal computer.

Figure 1.25

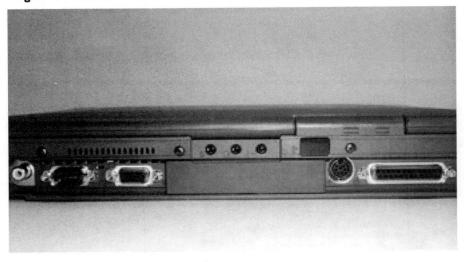

The ports on a notebook computer.

Figure 1.26

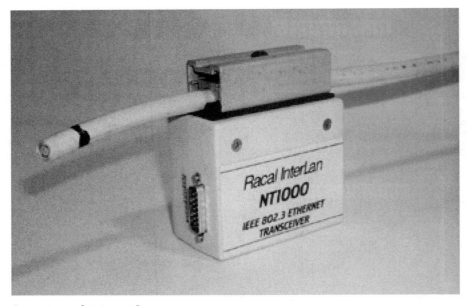

An external transceiver.

NIC Connectors

The type of cable media you choose for your network usually dictates the type of network adapter or NIC you need to install. In turn, the NIC sets the type of connectors you must use to connect the network media to the NIC. Depending on the type of media you choose, you will need to match it to the connectors used for that cable type. You'll find more information on connectors in Chapter 2 along with some illustrations of the different connectors.

Bandwidth is an issue for any network, whether it is the internal network of General Motors or your home network. Any time networking is discussed these days, and especially when the discussion involves the Internet, the topic is often bandwidth. You can never have enough.

Baseband Versus Broadband

Your home network is, or will be, a baseband network. Baseband networks use just one communications channel to send digital data over a line. Don't worry about what this means, just understand that all Ethernets, like nearly all LANs, are baseband networks.

You may have also heard of broadband networks, which use analog signaling that uses a wide range of frequencies to send data. It is possible that your office's WAN uses broadband services at some point.

Cable Media and Bandwidth

Bandwidth and the data speed supported by the network media are synonymous. In fact, bandwidth is expressed as the amount of data (in bits) that the cable can nominally transmit in 1 second. As we have mentioned before, the network you will build using the information in Chapter 3 is an Ethernet network. In terms of bandwidth this means is that your network will have a bandwidth of 10 or 100 Mbps, assuming you are not installing fiber optic cabling. The bandwidth of your network is determined by the cable type in use and the supporting connectivity devices managing the network's flow.

As listed in Table 1.1, each cable type has different performance and bandwidth characteristics. Because you are using UTP cable to install your home network, your bandwidth is likely to be 10 Mbps. This should be enough bandwidth to support up to ten workstations on the network. If you are concerned about your network's speed, consider the fact that your modem, which you use to connect your home network to the Internet, runs at only 56 Kbps. If your network is supporting ten nodes, each node is seeing, on average, around 5 Mbps of bandwidth, or around ten times more bandwidth than the modem provides.

Table 1.1
Ethernet Cable Media Characteristics

Cable type	Bandwidth (Mbps)	Segment length (m/ft)
Thin coaxial	10	185 /607
Thick coaxial	10	500/1,640
UTP	10 – 100	100 /328
STP	4 – 1000	100/328
Fiber optic	100 – 10,000	2000/6562

As indicated in Table 1.1, each type of Ethernet cable media also has a maximum length at which attenuation (when the transmitted signal begins to fade in strength) kicks in and the signal must be regenerated or it will be lost or garbled. This length should be considered the maximum length between workstations directly connected by network media on your network. Unless you have an extremely long house or plan to leave a long length of cable rolled up under your floor, you should have no problems with attenuation or the length of your cable segments.

10BaseT

One more bit of information before we move on to the tasks of actually building your home network, beginning in Chapter 2. You may run into the designation of *10BaseT* used in conjunction with UTP cable and Ethernet NICs. This is a shorthand way of saying that a cable or device is for a 10-Mbps baseband twisted-pair network. The "10" stands for 10 Mbps, "Base" stands for baseband signaling, and "T" stands for the twisted pair. UTP cable is also referred to as 10BaseT cable.

There are several other similar designations used for other technologies, not all of which follow the exact scheme or meaning as the 10BaseT designator. For example, thin coaxial cable is also known as 10Base2, which is a 10 Mbps baseband network with segment distance limits of 185 (close to 200, indicated by "2"). Likewise, 10Base5, the designator for thick coaxial cable, is a 10 Mbps baseband network with maximum segment lengths of 500.

There are also some higher-value designations. For example, 100BaseT is a 100-Mbps baseband twisted-pair network, and 100BaseF is a fiber optic network with 100 Mbps of bandwidth.

You're not ready to start building the network just yet. First you will need to purchase the components needed to build your network. In Chapter 2, we will examine the specifics of the cable and other network devices needed to make your home or office network function properly and reliably.

We hope this review of networking terms has helped you understand all of the jargon just a little.

Now on to the next step—buying the network components.

Gathering the Parts

The first step in building any network is to determine the purpose of the network. The purposes of a home network are really not much different than those of a corporate network: sharing data resources, collaboration on projects, or sharing hardware devices. It is not unusual for some home networks to be built because the owner just wants to do it, but in most cases there is a real purpose to the network. The cost of installing a home network is much lower than that of a printer or other high-cost peripheral device that can be easily shared over a network. So, even if you really just want to create a home network for the sake of doing it, there are real benefits to be realized.

With the purpose of the network decided, such as sharing the printer or modem, the next step is to decide on the topology, technology, and objectives you wish your network to use. In contrast to a corporate network, where this can be a complex and difficult decision, home networks are fairly standardized by the type and number of affordable components available for use. Unless you plan to install five or more nodes, you should plan on installing a peer-to-peer Ethernet network over UTP cabling. Beyond five nodes, the choice to install a server-based or client/server network is really a matter of preference, but beyond ten nodes, it is really a matter of necessity. If your home network is like most, it will have two, three, or maybe four nodes: two computers, a printer, and perhaps another shared device, such as a scanner, second printer, or fax machine. The network used as a model in this book is a three-node network with two computers and a printer.

Deciding on how large a home network is to be is usually determined by cost and complexity. One definitely is affected by the other. The more complex the network, the more it usually will cost. Our advise is, and we're sure you've never heard this before, "Keep it simple!"

Creating Your Shopping List

When you start to build a home network, the primary components of the network, your personal computers, are already in place. Therefore the focus of your networking project is the components you need to connect up your computers. From Chapter 1, you know that your shopping list must include network adapters for each of your computers, UTP cabling and Ethernet connectors, and possibly a hub to connect everything together. However, you may still be a little apprehensive about striking out on your network components shopping trip. To help you prepare for this expedition, the following sections examine the issues, considerations, and choices you will face in creating your shopping list and then choosing the components to buy.

Where to Start
Whether you start with the network adapter or the cable media is a kind of chicken-and-egg dilemma. Should you decide on the cable media that is best for your physical situation or should you settle on the type of network adapters first and then use the type of cabling they prescribe or will adapt to? Good question! However, we recommend that you start with the network adapters because there are often more restrictions on them than on the cabling.

As indicated earlier, the network we will be building in this book is a 10BaseT Ethernet network using UTP cabling. One reason we have chosen to demonstrate this type of network installation is that it is by far the most common type installed in homes and small offices. Another good reason for this type of network is that its components are relatively inexpensive, easily installed, and usually successful on the first try. What shouldn't be at issue here is the 10BaseT and Ethernet parts of the network configuration. What you may wish to change are the network adapters and cable media used to create the network.

Network Adapters

There is a variety of different network adapters on the market, each supporting a possible variety of cable media types, which you can choose from to build your network. There are internal adapters and external adapters. Some adapters support UTP cabling, and others support the telephone or electrical power lines in your home. There are even network adapters that support wireless connections.

INTERNAL NETWORK ADAPTERS   The most commonly used network adapter is the internal NIC. Figure 2.1 shows an Ethernet 10BaseT NIC of the type used in the majority of installed home networks.

Figure 2.1

A common Ethernet network interface card.

The type, or types, of expansion slots available inside your computer is the primary criterion for selecting the correct NIC for your network. The type of slot available is determined by its expansion bus architecture. The most common types of expansion slots available on Pentium computers support the ISA and PCI bus architectures. You may also find EISA and perhaps even a Video Electronics Standards Association local bus (VESA) slot on your computer, but these are more common in older and brand-name, proprietary computers. Figures 2.2 and 2.3 show expansion slots for ISA and PCI cards, respectively. Figure 2.4 illustrates the edge connectors for these and other expansion bus cards.

Figure 2.2

ISA expansion slot.

If you are unable to determine which type of expansion slot is open on your computer's motherboard, consult the documentation for your system, contact your supplier, or visit the manufacturer's website.

Once you have determined the type of open slot or slots on your computer's motherboard, you will know the type of NIC card you need. If the open slot is a PCI slot, which should be the case on most newer computers, then you know that you need a PCI NIC. If you have an ISA slot, which is also quite common, then your shopping list will include an ISA NIC. If you have one of each available, then it is really a matter of choice.

Both PCI and ISA NICs are usually available and run about the same cost, about $8.00 to about $50.00 depending on the cable media supported and the features of the card. A very good site to find prices of network adapters of any type is www.pricewatch.com, shown in Figure 2.5. Look for 10BaseT network adapters under networking products.

Figure 2.3

PCI expansion slot.

Figure 2.4

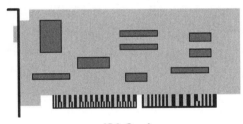

ISA Card

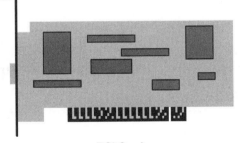

PCI Card

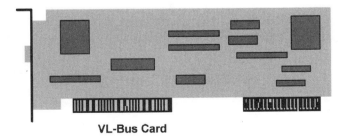

VL-Bus Card

Common expansion card formats.

Figure 2.5

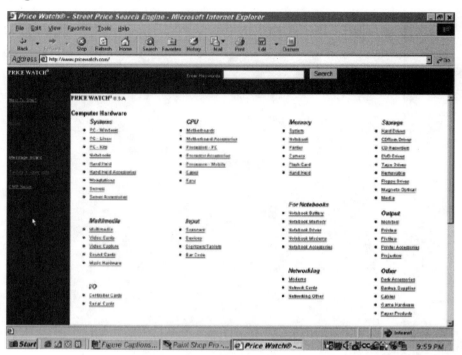

Pricewatch.Com is a good place to check prices for network components.

EXTERNAL NETWORK ADAPTERS   New to the home networking marketplace are a number of network adapters that are installed externally to the computer and plug into one of the computer's standard I/O ports. There are network adapters that plug into and will share the parallel port on your computer, which is normally used for your printer. Another network adapter type that is growing in popularity uses the computer's USB port. Not all computers have a USB port, but it has become common over the past year or so, especially on Pentium II and III systems.

External network adapters typically come in kits that also contain the cabling and device drivers you will need to install and configure your network. This type of network adapter quite commonly also involves the use of alternative network media. For example, Intelogis makes a kit called the PassPort Network that uses your home's electrical wiring to create a network. The network adapters plug into your power outlets and then connect to your computer using the parallel port. Figure 2.6 shows PassPort adapter.

Another example is the AnyPoint network adapter from Intel. It uses your home's built-in telephone wiring to create a network. The network adapters are free-standing and connect to the RJ-11 telephone jack plugs on your wall and to the USB port on your computer. Figure 2.7 shows an AnyPoint network adapter.

Figure 2.6

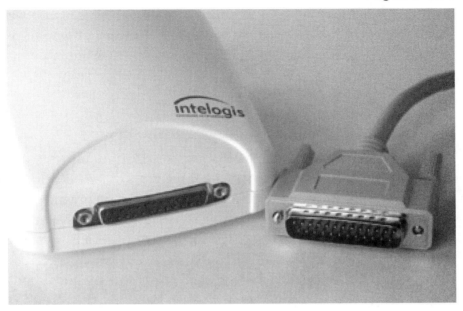

A network adapter that uses the computer's parallel port.

Figure 2.7

A USB network adapter.

USB adapters range in price from about $25 to about $60 depending on quality, features, and technical support available. Kits such as the PassPort network adapter cost about $80 for three devices.

Naturally, networking kits, like those mentioned above, cost more than single network adapters, especially internal NICs, but they usually make up for the price in friendliness. However, if you have enough friends but not enough money, then you may want to put in the effort, save the money, and use internal network adapters.

NIC Configuration

When buying a network adapter, be sure to ask how the network interface card is configured. There are three ways that a NIC can be configured, with software (in the form of an installation program that comes with the card), using dual inline packaging (DIP) switch blocks, or with jumper block settings. Figure 2.8 shows a DIP switch block, and Figure 2.9 shows jumper blocks on a network card. Regardless of the process used, the system resource assignments and transceiver types on the adapter must be set. Naturally, the best of all worlds is to have a plug-and-play adapter that also comes with an installation program. However, there are non–plug-and-play NICs that, although they have set-up software, occasionally still require a hardware adjustment through a DIP switch or jumper. If your NICs are configured manually, there are a number of settings that you need to configure. We will discuss these settings in Chapter 3.

Figure 2.8

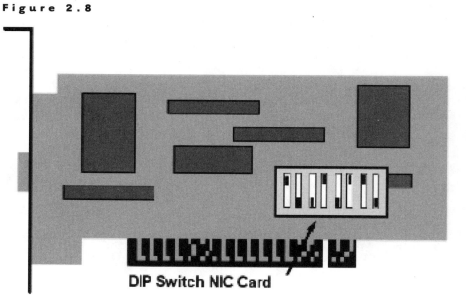

DIP Switch NIC Card

A DIP switch block.

Figure 2.9

Jumper blocks on a NIC.

Portable Computer Network Adapters

It is entirely possible, and actually quite common, to include a portable computer, such as a notebook, in your network. There is a wide range of easily installed and affordable network adapters available for notebook computers. The type of network adapter used in a notebook computer is a PCMCIA card, which is, thankfully, also becoming known as a PC card.

A PC card network adapter slides into a slot, or one of a pair of slots, on the side of the notebook computer. Figure 2.10 shows a PC card network adapter. Notice the attached plug adapter, called a *dongle*, that is used to connect the network cable to the PC card.

Figure 2.11 shows the PC card network adapter being installed in a notebook computer. PC cards are plug-and-play devices that can be "hot-swapped," which means that they can be installed or removed while the computer is running and do not require the computer to be restarted when installed to be activated and available for use.

So, if you have a notebook or other portable computer to be included in your network, plan on adding an Ethernet 10BaseT PCMCIA, or PC card, to you shopping list.

Figure 2.10

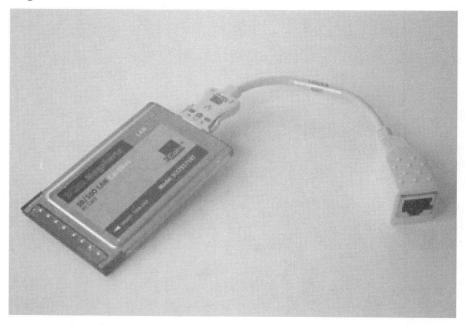

PCMCIA or PC Card network adapter.

Figure 2.11

The PC Card network adapter is installed in a PCMCIA slot.

Because we have decided that the network we are building is to be an Ethernet 10BaseT network, our choices for network media have already been narrowed down to one type—UTP. The choice to use copper wiring is a simple one. Copper twisted-pair wiring is inexpensive, easy to work with, and readily available. Other cabling choices, such as coaxial cable or fiber optic, can be difficult to get in shorter lengths, difficult to work with, and are generally more expensive. Unless you can find the right amount of coaxial cable, and thin coaxial cable is preferred over thick coaxial cable, and the network adapters and transceivers needed at a reasonable price, your best bet is to use UTP wiring, shown in Figure 2.12.

Figure 2.12

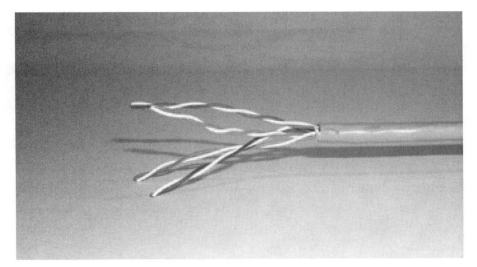

UTP wire.

UTP versus STP

Now that the decision has been made to use twisted-pair copper wire, why use UTP wiring and not STP wiring? There are advantages and disadvantages to both.

Twisted-pair cable is not a recent development. In fact, it has been around for quite a while. Early telephone systems used twisted-pair cable, and you'll find twisted-pair cable in just about every building today being used for telephone and other signals. UTP and STP cable use eight wires. They are often mistaken for telephone cable, which connects only four wires.

What has changed over the years is the amount of bandwidth that twisted-pair cabling can support and the amount of electrical interference the cable can withstand. The cable used with the early telephone system carried 1200 bits per second, but with new technology, twisted-pair cable now supports more than 100 million bits per second. Today's cable must also contend with many more new forms of electrical interference than did the earlier cable.

TWISTED-PAIR WIRING CONSTRUCTION Twisted-pair wiring typically consists of eight copper wires, each insulated in a color-code plastic coating. These wires are divided into four sets of two copper wires that are twisted together to form a twisted pair, which is where this cable type gets its name. The four twisted pairs are then wrapped by an outer jacket of rubber or plastic to form twisted-pair cable. The number of twists per inch is different in adjacent pairs, thereby minimizing the possibility of electrical interference between the pairs.

When installing any type of twisted-pair cabling, you must avoid situations where the cable may be subjected to *electromagnetic interference* (EMI). EMI, also called electrical noise, is emitted by such things as electric motors, electrical power lines, or high-powered radio or radar signals in your vicinity. EMI is what you hear from your radio or television whenever the vacuum cleaner is running. So, when you install the network cable in your home, avoid running it next to or near your soft-drink vending machine, your radar transmitter, your walk-in freezer, or any other high-EMI device you may have.

SHIELDED TWISTED-PAIR STP cables, shown in Figure 2.13, include a metal shield that is wrapped around the twisted-pair bundle to minimize EMI problems. It would seem that in areas where EMI may be a problem that STP cable is the solution—well, not exactly. If it is properly grounded, the STP cable's shield acts like an antenna, attracting any stray electrical noise away from the twisted-pair wires. If the cable is not properly grounded or becomes pierced or broken, the shielding may actually increase the EMI problem.

Another STP drawback is that the shield is usually a thick braided metal fabric that makes the overall cable thicker than the UTP and, because of its special handling and grounding requirements, relatively more difficult to install. There are variations of STP, called *screened twisted pair* (ScTP) and *foil twisted pair* (FTP), that use a thin foil sheath in place of the thicker braided sheath. They are thinner and less expensive than braided STP cable, but handling can be a problem because the foil is easier to tear, thereby eliminating the shielding benefit.

Figure 2.13

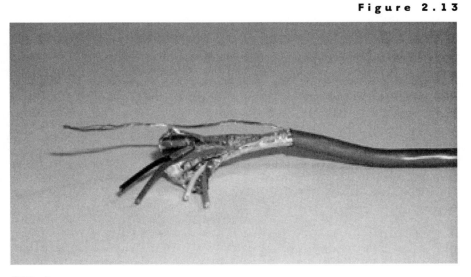

STP wire.

UNSHIELDED TWIST–PAIR   UTP cable, shown in Figure 2.12, does not include any metallic shielding to block electrical interference. Instead, it uses a noise balancing scheme that cancels out EMI in the wire. Care must still be taken to avoid placing UTP wire near sources of EMI. However, if you use a quality UTP wire and install it properly, UTP has several advantages over STP cable: it is lighter, thinner, and more flexible, and it costs less.

UTP is the most commonly used network cable. It provides the most installation flexibility and ease of maintenance of any of the cabling media available for home use. We will discuss its installation process and how to avoid performance problems in Chapter 3.

Cable Categories

UTP cable is grouped into five categories, or "Cats" as you will hear techies refer to them (as in Cat 3 or Cat 5):

■ Category 3, a.k.a. Cat 3, cable is a four-pair cable that supports bandwidth up to 10 Mbps and is the minimum standard for 10BaseT networks. If you can find it, it will work for your home network.

■ Cat 4 is a four-wire cable, commonly used in 16 Mbps token ring networks. We don't recommend you spend your money on this type of cable.

■ Cat 5, which is also a four-wire cable, supports bandwidths up to 100 Mbps. You may be advised to used Cat 5 along the way, but unless it is already included in a networking kit, you may want to save your money and use Cat 3 instead.

Just to satisfy your curiosity, Cat 1 and 2 cables are not used in networking.

Plenum Versus PVC

The outer jacket of UTP cabling is usually PVC plastic, which is generally fine for most installations. However, some building codes require the use of plenum cabling. PVC cable sheaths can produce toxic fumes when on fire. Plenum cables, which are made from Teflon, do not produce toxic fumes and are required in certain usage situations. Plenum cable is more expensive than ordinary cabling, but it may be required by your local building code or you may want it for your own peace of mind.

If you plan on installing your own connectors, then finding boxes of 250 feet or more of plenum cable is rather easy. However, it may be difficult to find UTP plenum cable in cut lengths already terminated with RJ-45 connectors. Check with your local computer supply store for help.

UTP Connectors

Once you have decided on the cable type you will be using for your home network, you must get the connectors that are used for that cable. The demonstration network you will be installing (Chapter 3) uses UTP. For that reason, we discuss UTP connectors first. However, just for your information or if you have decided to use coaxial media, we also discuss the connectors used for that medium.

If you are not buying cables already terminated with connectors and want to expand the experience of installing your home network to include putting the connectors on the cable, then you will also need to purchase a few tools. There is a section that lists the tools needed to attach connectors and install cabling later in this chapter.

RJ-45   The connector used for UTP cable is the registered jack 45 (RJ-45) connector. The RJ-45 connector is a slightly larger version of the connector (RJ-11) used to plug your telephone into the wall jack. An RJ-45 connector connects eight wires from the UTP cable as opposed to the RJ-11 connector that connects only four wires for the telephone system. Figure 2.14 shows an RJ-45 connector attached to UTP wire.

Figure 2.14

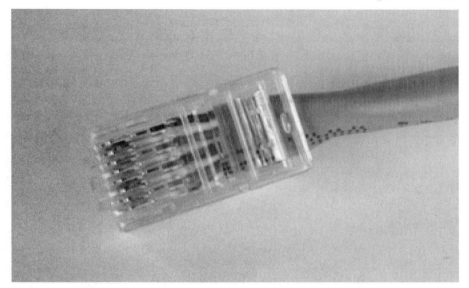

An RJ-45 connector.

RJ-11   Network adapters that create your home network by using the existing telephone wiring installed in the walls of your home connect to a phone jack with an RJ-11 connector. This is the common four-wire connector used in nearly all newer telephone installations. Figure 2.15 shows an RJ-11 connector attached to an Intel AnyPort Phoneline network adapter.

Figure 2.15

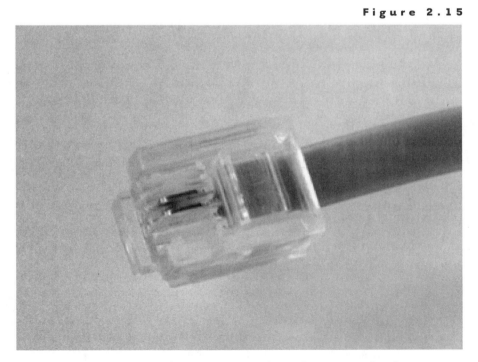

An RJ-11 connector used to connect a phone line network adapter.

BNC CONNECTOR   Both thin and thick coaxial cables can use a special connector set called a BNC connector, but BNC connectors are much more commonly used on thin coaxial cable. There are many versions of what the BNC abbreviation means, but Bayonet Neil-Concelman or British Naval Connector are the most commonly used. It really doesn't matter; the connector is simply called a BNC connector. Figure 2.16 shows a BNC connector on a network cable.

Figure 2.16

A BNC connector on a network cable.

Coaxial cable is connected to nodes in a daisy-chain fashion. Each workstation is connected to the next by a segment of coaxial cable. Each end of the coaxial cable segment is terminated with what is called a *bayonet connector*. Look at the end of the coaxial cable that attaches to your cable box or television set to see what this connector looks like. The cable segments are then attached to one side of the BNC T-connector, shown in Figure 2.17. If there are other workstations beyond the current workstation, then a connecting cable segment is attached to the other side of the T-connector to create the next network segment. If there are no more workstations in the network, then the cable must be terminated. Most of the T-connectors available are self-terminating, but if you wish to use coaxial cable for your network, make sure you know how the connectors you buy are terminated.

VAMPIRE TAPS   Thick coaxial cable typically uses a cable connection, called a *vampire tap*, that clamps into and pierces the cable to make its connection, as shown in Figure 2.18. Vampire taps attach thick Ethernet transceivers to the coaxial cable. The transceiver is

Build Your Own Home Network

then attached to the network adapter installed in the computer with a patch cord and an attachment unit interface (AUI) plug. The use of the vampire tap and AUI patch cable eliminates the need to cut the cable and install BNC connectors to each end. Remember that your network adapter must also match the type of connectors used with the cabling.

Figure 2.17

BNC T-Connector.

INFORMATION SOURCE   There are a number of very good Web sites on the Internet that have information on cabling and connectors. One especially good site is the Hardware Book site, maintained by Joakim Ögren in Sweden (www.hwb.acc.umu.se).

Tools and Supplies

When making up cabling for your home network, you have a choice. You can buy cabling in bulk and terminate each segment (which is very likely only one or two segments anyway) with the appropriate connector, or you can purchase cable in specific lengths already terminated with the right connector (which may also carry a guarantee). It really depends on the amount of time, effort, and adventure you wish to invest in the project. Cost is not a significant factor, when you consider your time and the cost of the tools you must buy.

Figure 2.18

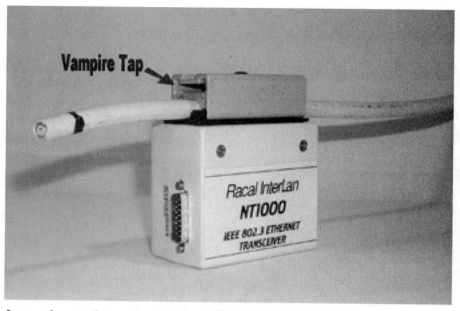

A vampire tap is used to connect an external transceiver.

Crimper

Depending on the type of cable medium you are using in your network, if you plan on making up your own cabling, you will need a crimper:

- An RJ crimper is used to set RJ-11 and RJ-45 connectors to the end of the UTP cable. If you are dead set on making up your own cables, get a good crimper with the correct modules for the connectors you are using. You may be able to find one at your local electrical supply store, but your best bet is through an online supplier, such as Milestek or Parts Express. Good sets start at around $50. Figure 2.19 shows what is called a universal crimper.

- Only if you are actually planning to make up thin coaxial cables will you need a coaxial cable crimper and BNC connector modules. Look for them online at suppliers such as Milestek for around $20.

Don't forget to buy enough of the appropriate connectors for your network, including a few extra connectors to cover your learning curve in attaching the connector to the wire. On the same note, always add an extra foot or two to each cable length to allow for connector mistakes and errors that must be cut off and reattached.

Figure 2.19

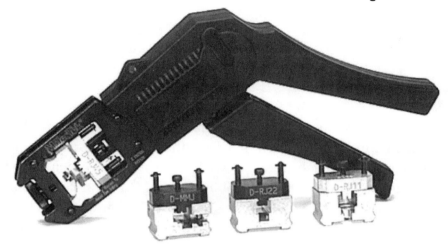

A universal crimper is used to connect RJ-25 connectors to UTP wire.

Other Tools You May Need

As we will discuss further in Chapter 3, at some point you will need to decide where you will run your cable. Are you planning to fish it through the walls, run it under the floor, or above the ceiling? Regardless, you may need some additional tools to help you place the cable where you want it. Here are some of the tools you may want to consider.

■ Electrician's scissors are used to trim and strip the insulation from the individual wires in the UTP cable.

■ Electric (cordless is better) drill with a set of spade drill bits to be used to place holes in the floor, walls, or ceiling.

■ Eye goggles or protection, especially if you plan to drill overhead, but something you should wear whenever you operate drills or cutting tools.

■ A stud finder and an electrician's fish tape are needed only if you plan to install your cable in a preexisting conduit in your home or office walls. As most homes do not have conduit systems, these tools are optional. However, some newer homes do have sound or intercom systems placed in a small-diameter conduit, so this may be something to consider.

■ A first-aid kit is certainly something you should have available anytime you are working with tools.

A good Web site to visit for information on networking tools and supplies is www.milestek.com.

Summary

What it all boils down to is that the materials and tools you need for the job of building your own home or office network really depend on you and how much work you wish to do and how much money you want to spend. Using UTP cabling in precut and preterminated lengths can really simplify the task. However, if you wish this to be a deeper learning experience, you can purchase all of the materials and create your own cables. In any case, you'll need the appropriate network adapters for the cable and connector types you've decided to use.

You may also need some additional tools. Our best advice is that, before you buy a tool, be sure you understand why it is needed and exactly how it is used.

CHAPTER 3

Installing Your New Network

Like most other construction projects, building your own home network requires careful planning. There are many things you need to consider before you start, each of which will prevent problems after you've started. There is an old programming joke that applies here: "I'll start programming and you go find out what they want." The joke is that we are always so eager to get on with it, that we are willing to risk even redoing a project. Like our eager programmer, you are probably just as eager to begin installing your new network, the devil is definitely in the details, and unless you plan your network; but it may result in unnecessary steps, wasted time, and misspent money.

Before you begin building your network, you should lay out a thorough floor plan and gather the tools and materials you need to complete your network. If you don't plan just what you are trying to accomplish, you may get halfway only to find that what you have in mind is no longer possible and that you will have to start over. Trust us, it is far better that you spend some time planning out what you want your network to be and what you need to do before you begin drilling holes, climbing ladders, and pulling cable. The need to plan your network cannot be stressed too much: a byte of planning is worth a megabyte of patching—oh well, we're sure you get the idea.

Planning to Succeed

Even if your goal is a network much more sophisticated than the one we're building with this book, we recommend that, before you start installing your network, you read through all of the installation steps in this chapter. Despite your experience level, there are always some things you may have forgotten, several things everyone should consider, and some things you may want to reconsider before deciding on an approach that best suits your particular networking needs.

Here is a list of the key elements that you should absolutely consider when planning your network:

- **The operating system:** The operating system, or operating systems, installed on the computers to be networked may make the job easier or more complex.

- **Computer placement:** Where your computers are physically placed can have an affect on your network and the path and method used to interconnect them.

- **Number of computers:** There are effective limits to the number of computers and other devices that should be included in a home network before it turns into something else altogether.

- **Peer-to-peer versus client-server:** In this book and especially in this chapter, we focus on the construction of a peer-to-peer network. If you wish to build something more than that, the setup and layout may be totally different.

- **Internet sharing:** If you plan to share the Internet across your network, there are some special configuration steps to be performed.

In each of these areas, you have choices available and the choices you make can impact the choices you have in other areas. For example, if you decide that you want to install a peer-to-peer network with directly connected workstations running Windows 98 SE and Internet sharing, then you won't need that big and expensive router you had your eye, and heart, set on using. In this example, about all that is left to be worked out is where you want to place the stations in your house. However, if your choice is to install a fully redundant client/server network supporting an intranet with access to multiple paths to the Internet; first of all, you have the wrong book, and second, you may want to consider that this network is just a bit more than most home networks require.

The Operating System

There are several versions of the Windows operating system available that can be used on your network's computers, all of which will work just fine. In fact, you really aren't required to use Windows at all. A home network will work equally well with the Linux operating system. We've even included some instructions at the end of this chapter, just in case you were curious about what would be involved to install that operating system instead.

We have chosen to use Windows as the operating system for our model network for many reasons, not least of which is its popularity. We are using Windows 98 SE (Figure 3.1), but, whichever version of Windows you use, we recommend that you use the same version on all of the computers in your network. Having the same operating system throughout your network is the best advice we can give you for making your network easier to manage and administer.

DETERMINING THE OPERATING SYSTEM VERSION ON YOUR COMPUTER   To determine which version of Windows is installed on your computer, perform the following steps:

1. On the Windows Desktop, shown in Figure 3.1, right-click on the My Computer icon. This will display a short-cut menu for My Computer, as shown in Figure 3.2.

2. Choose the Properties option by clicking on it. This displays the Properties window shown in Figure 3.3.

3. Click on the General tab (it should be the default, which means the one selected automatically); on it you will find information something like that shown in Figure 3.4:

   a. Microsoft Windows 98

   b. 4.10.1998

Figure 3.1

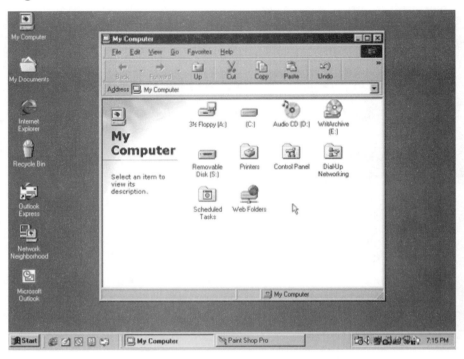

The Windows desktop.

Figure 3.2

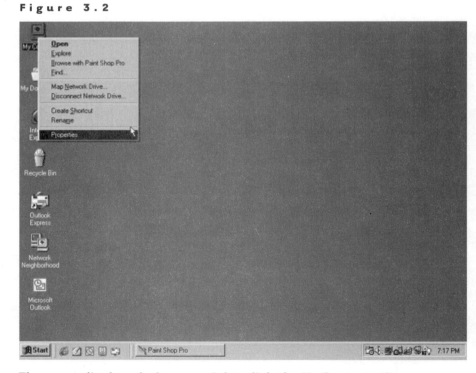

The menu displayed when you right-click the My Computer icon.

Figure 3.3

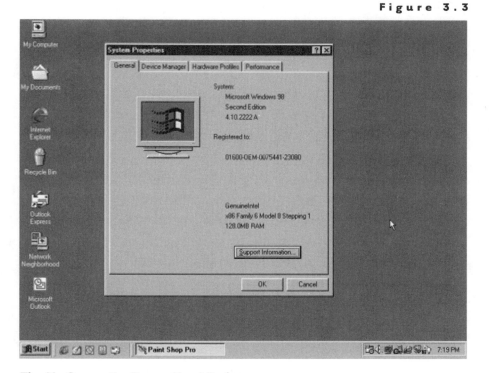

The My Computer Properties Window.

Figure 3.4

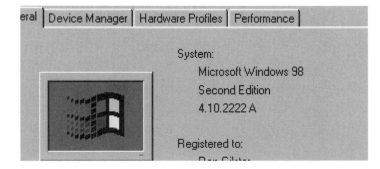

The System Information on the My Computer Properties Window.

These two bits of information tell you that you are using Microsoft Windows 98, version 4.10.1998.

Internet Sharing

One of the benefits to networking your home computers is that you can share access to the Internet through one phone line and one Internet access account. Without a network, only one of your home computers can connect to the Internet over a single phone line and

Internet access account. If you wish each of the nodes on your network have access to the Internet, you have two options: a proxy server with modems or through the Windows 98 Internet Sharing feature.

USING A PROXY SERVER   An easy way to share access to the Internet on a network is to purchase and install a device called a *proxy server* on your network. A proxy server, which can be either a piece of hardware or software, manages the connection to the Internet and connects and disconnects from the network as required to provide access to all network nodes. A proxy server also caches, or stores for future access, Web pages and documents, downloaded by network users to speed up the download process. Caching is a process that stores Web documents so that future requests of the same document can be fulfilled from the cache without the need to access the Internet. Caching on a proxy server is often able to fill a request for a frequently accessed Web page without making a dial-up connection. Most proxy servers include caching as a standard feature.

The most common type of proxy server connects to your computer's serial port in place of an external modem. Some proxy server models have one or more modems built into them, such as the one shown in Figure 3.5, and on other models external modems are plugged into the proxy server. Figure 3.5 shows a single-line proxy server.

Figure 3.5

A single-line proxy server.

USING WINDOWS 98 INTERNET SHARING   Windows 98 provides a feature that allows you to share a single Internet connection among the nodes on a home network. To take advantage of these feature, one of your computers needs to be designated and set up as the connection sharing computer. This computer receives requests for Internet access from the other nodes on the network and routes them to the Internet. Windows 98 Internet Sharing can also be used to allow external Internet users to access any Web, e-mail, or game servers you may set up on your internal network.

USING THE INTERNET CONNECTION WIZARD   A real handy feature, the Internet Connection wizard, helps you set up your computer to share an Internet connection. It is accessed from the Start → Programs → Accessories → Internet Tools menus on the Windows Desktop. Figure 3.6 shows the opening window of the Internet Connection Wizard. We will discuss this a little more later in this chapter.

Figure 3.6

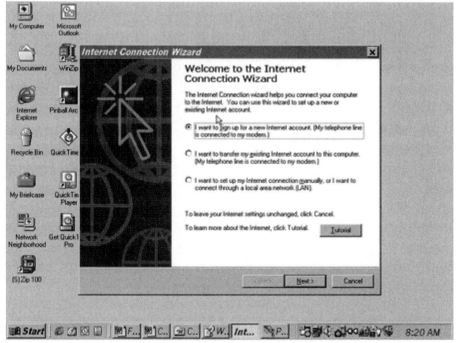

The Windows 98 Internet Sharing Wizard.

Computer Placement
It may sound somewhat obvious, but you need to decide just where you want to place your computers. It may not seem to be all that big

of a deal, but you really need to be fairly specific about where, in what room, and where in the room each computer is to be situated. Think about where these placements are in relation to one another. The most ideal situation is when all of the computers on your network are to be located in the same room, but if you are not that lucky this time, then take note of the conditions that will affect your placements.

What conditions are those? Is there a brick wall between the computers? A brick wall will make drilling a hole for the network cables just a bit more difficult. Will you need to drill a hole through a ceiling to reach into a room above it? Are the rooms even in the same building, such as an office above a detached garage and a children's study room in the basement of the house? There are as many variables to consider as there are types of house architectures, so we will try to keep our examples simple but at the same time fairly representative of reality. So that you can see most of the steps used to locate the computers and the cabling, we won't be placing our computers in the same room.

Here are a few other things you should consider when placing your computers:

- Is the desired spot too close to a heating vent? Your computer may overheat if it is too close to a heat source.

- Don't place your computer near water outlets or you may make a "shocking" discovery.

- Are there enough electrical outlets to support your computer and any other peripherals (printer, scanner, etc.) you may attach to your computer?

- Is there a phone line located nearby for you to connect one of the computers to access the Internet?

These are probably the most important considerations of deciding where to locate the computers of your network. These things may seem to be common sense, but that's the point—use your common sense and don't take chances that may endanger you or your computers.

Number of Computers

Just in case you've forgotten how many computers you own, count the number of computers you want to add to your home network. For most of home networks, including ours, this should be a fairly simple task. The answer is most likely two or three. The number of computers involved in this project determines the number of network interface cards, cables, and other connectivity tools you need to purchase. The number of nodes on the network also decides the size of the hub needed, if you plan to use one. Luckily, hubs come in various sizes ranging from 4, shown in Figure 3.7, to 16 or more connections.

Figure 3.7

A five-port hub.

Path Layout

The next step in building your home network is determining the path to run the Ethernet cabling that will physically connect your computers together. This will show how well you have chosen your computer placements. A simple but effective method to designing your cable placements is to take a notepad and pencil and walk from one desired computer placement to the other. As you go, sketch the floor plan of your house and make a special note of any obstacle that will need to be dealt with, such as walls, pipes, furniture, trees, and so on.

Luckily, Ethernet cabling is generally flexible. It can be placed along walls and curved around corners from one room to the next. If you plan to install your cable on the floor along wall edges, it is a good idea to consider securing the cable with plastic cable management clips. Securing your cable this way (Figure 3.8), eliminates the hazards of someone tripping over the cable or the cable being snagged by moving objects, such as children, pets, recliners, doors, filing cabinets, or exercise equipment (it could happen). Also note that your cabling should not be bent at sharp angles, crushed, crimped, stapled through, tread on repeatedly (unless protected with a traffic cable cover), or exposed to other damaging possibilities.

Figure 3.8

A network cable secured with cable management clips.

Another simple method of cabling your network is to run the cables through the crawl space beneath your house or on the underside of a floor to an unfinished basement. With this method, you are less likely to encounter as many obstacles as you would if you ran the cable along your baseboards. However, you need to be careful when installing the cable around heating and air-conditioning ducts, central vacuum systems, and electrical wiring. Making use of the crawl space beneath your floor merely requires that a hole be drilled through the floor near the desired location of each computer. Drilling a hole through the floor is okay, provided that you drill holes that are just big enough for the wire and that you either own the home or have the permission of the owner. Another consideration is that, if you do run the cable under the house in the crawl space, be sure to secure the cable with cable ties or cable management clips, so that it will not interfere with any future repair work you may need on your heating, plumbing, or electrical work in the same space.

Remember, "A byte of prevention is worth a megabyte of patching."

Path Measurement

PART 1   After you have completed your first walk along the cable path, with your notepad and pencil still in hand, walk the cable path again. This time take along a measuring tape to begin measuring the actual path of the cable. Don't forget that if the computer will be located on a desk, you need to include the distance from the back of the computer case to the ground, or ceiling, that the wire will be traveling through or along. Measure around corners, up walls, down walls, and through floors (estimate these measurements). Do not cut corners, no pun intended, when measuring for cable length.

PART 2   Now that you've completed two trips along the cable path and have verified the path and measured its distances, use your measuring tape to remeasure the cable path one more time. Yes, you've already measured and this is a duplicate step, but remember what you learned in shop, sewing, cooking, or science class; "Measure twice and cut once."

Once you've verified your measurements, add up the measurements to find the total length of cable needed to connect your computers to the network. If, for some reason, the second measurements differ from the first measurements, our advice is to remeasure carefully and compare to see which of the previous measurements was correct. If you continue to get different lengths, keep on measuring; sooner or later, you will see a trend.

Add an additional 10 feet to the longest of your measurements to provide for extra cable. The extra length helps avoid any surprises in the cable length resulting from obstacles not easily measured, such as bends, corners, and stairs. We like to call this extra 10 feet (or so) the "oops!" length of cable. Circumstances never fail that, once you get your cable installed from one computer location to another, you fall short about 6 inches and declare "oops!" or some other more colorful expletive.

Your backup option to the "oops!" length is the "fudge" option. To exercise this option, you simply move your second computer closer so that the cable fits. However, if you plan and measure correctly, you should not need to exercise this option. If your computers are located in the same room, you probably don't need to add the whole 10 feet of the "oops!" factor, but don't eliminate it completely; just adjust accordingly.

Don't forget, Ethernet cable does not stretch, nor should you attempt to stretch it, because you will damage the wiring inside of the cable.

Network Interface Cards

Another decision that needs to be made early in your planning concerns the type of NIC you need for your computers. Some newer computers, usually high-end, more expensive models, now come with a NIC already installed. If this is the case, be sure you know the manufacturer and type of card installed in your computer.

If you need to install a NIC in any or all of your computers, you will first need to check all of your computers for the types of expansion slots available in each. It is perfectly fine if your network computers use different bus architectures (meaning different expansion card types), but using the same type of expansion slot for all of your NICs is definitely preferred.

Unless you are using the exact same brand and model of computers, you will need to be certain which type of NIC will fit into each computer. To find out the expansion slots available in a computer, follow these steps:

1. Turn the computer off and unplug it.

2. Remove the case from the system unit.

3. If you have an antistatic wrist strap, put it on and ground it to the inside of the case. If you don't have one, get one. For now, you can simply keep your hand in contact with one of the internal case parts, so that you remain grounded. Either way, be very careful not to touch anything inside at this point to avoid accidentally giving the computer a static shock and causing irreparable damage to any or all components in the computer.

4. Look at the motherboard; an example is shown in Figure 3.9. The motherboard is usually the largest circuit board inside the computer's case. Find the expansion card slots, as indicated on Figure 3.9. These are typically about 3 to 4 inches long with metal striping in them. The white plastic slots running parallel to each other are PCI slots (Figure 3.10), your expansion slot of choice. If there is one that does not have anything inserted into it, you will want to purchase a PCI NIC for this computer. If there are no PCI slots in your computer or if none are available, you want to look for black plastic slots (there may be several slots or only one). These slots are ISA slots, shown in Figure

3.11, and if one is available, this is your next choice. PCI and ISA NICs are the most common and less expensive, and you will be able to find them easily. When purchasing a NIC, it would be preferable to purchase one that is rated for 10/100 Mbps rather than one rated for only 10 Mbps or 100 Mbps. This gives you some flexibility to install or upgrade your network later to a higher and faster bandwidth.

Figure 3.9

A computer motherboard showing the expansion slots.

Figure 3.10

A PCI expansion slot.

Figure 3.11

An ISA expansion slot.

Purchasing Equipment

The time has come for you to go to your local computer supply store or online to your favorite e-commerce site to purchase the items required to build your own home network. If you have the time to wait for shipping, you may be able to save some money by shopping online, but your local computer supply store may have the items you need in stock and on their display shelves, which can save time.

We have compiled the items that should be on your network shopping list into the following list:

- **NICs** (one for each computer on your network) to fit the available slots you found in each computer as described in the section Network Interface Cards (Figure 3.12).

- **One Cat 5, "rolled" Ethernet cable with RJ-45 connectors already attached**, (Figure 3.13). You will need one length of cable long enough to reach the hub from each computer. For instance, if you are attaching three computers to your network, you will need three lengths of cable; for four computers, you will need four lengths of cable, and so on. The lengths should be equal to the path measurements described in parts 1 and 2 of the section Path Measurement." Don't forget to give yourself the additional 10 feet of "oops!" cable.

Figure 3.12

A network interface card (NIC).

By the way, a rolled cable is one that is capable of interconnecting two devices directly and has two of its inside wires reversed, or rolled, to create a crossover situation so that the computers communicate with each other over the same wires. Be sure you ask for a rolled cable when buying this item.

- **Plastic cable management clips.** You will want to purchase a cable clip (Figure 3.14) for every 18 inches or so of cable running along a baseboard if this is the option that you choose. If you are using them to secure your cable in a crawl space, you will not need to use as many and will need to purchase only one for every 4 feet of cable.

- **Proxy server.** If you have decided to connect your network to the Internet using a proxy server (see the section Using a Proxy Server earlier in the chapter), you may need to purchase this from the Internet or a full-service computer store that specializes in network equipment. Some popular brand names are Intel, 3Com, and Multi-Tech. If you are connecting over a standard modem or through a DSL connection, see Connecting with a DSL Service later in this chapter.

Figure 3.13

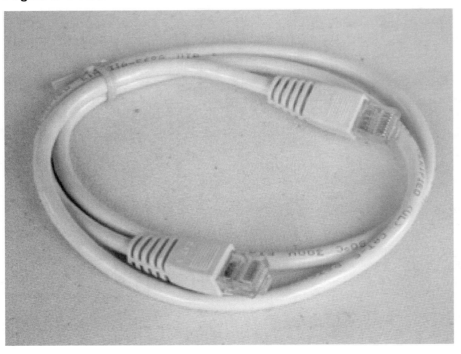

An Ethernet cable with RJ-45 connectors attached.

Figure 3.14

A cable management clip is used to guide the path of the cable.

■ **One 3½-inch floppy disk.** You will need this floppy if you plan to share an Internet connection on your network.

■ **Your Windows 98 CD-ROM disk.** You will need this to supply device driver and protocol files.

■ **A hub.** If you are connecting more than two computers or nodes to your network, you also need to purchase a hub. The hub must be matched to the speed (10 or 100 Mbps, or auto-sensing, which means that it can detect the speed of the network devices automatically) of the NICs and have enough ports to connect each computer on your network (and any other nodes you plan on connecting, such as a printer or scanner). It is better to buy a hub with a few extra ports beyond what you need immediately than to come up short at a later date when you decide to put a computer in every room of your house. Unfortunately, you won't be able to trade in your hub later.

Installing the Cable

As we've discussed earlier in this chapter, there are two options for installing network cable in your home. Your choice will depend on whether you can stand to see the cable running along the baseboards of your rooms and halls or wish to hide it under the floor. This assumes, of course, that you have a crawl space or basement in which to run the cable out of sight. An alternative to running the cable under the floor is running the cable above the ceiling. In any case, your choices are in sight and out of sight.

Drilling Instructions

If you are planning to place your cable along the baseboard in your home, you can skip this section, because you should not need to drill any holes. However, if you plan to hide your cables, you will need to drill holes and you will definitely need to add an electric drill and ⅛-inch and ⅜-inch drill bits to your tool list. We also strongly recommend that you always wear protective goggles when drilling and adhere to all safety recommendations included with your power tools.

■ Cut a 4- to 6-inch section of wire from a wire coat hanger with a pair of wire cutters. This piece of wire will be used as a guide for making sure your hole is in the best place.

■ Look over the room one more time before beginning to drill holes in the floor (or ceiling). Be sure this is what you want to do and perhaps even measure one more time. If you have already bought the cable, and there is a surprise in the measurements at this point, you may need to move the hole.

■ Drill a pilot hole just big enough (⅛ inch) to guide your piece of coat hanger through (Figure 3.15). The hole should be as close to a wall as possible and angled slightly toward the wall.

Figure 3.15

Drill a pilot hole so you can check the path of the cable.

■ Bend the hole guide wire slightly and then guide it through the hole, leaving it exposed above (and, one hopes, below) the floor (or ceiling) as shown in Figure 3.16.

■ Now go below the floor, that is, into the crawl space or basement (or above in the attic) and locate the hole guide wire marking the hole. If you cannot find it, it may be marking a hole inside a heating duct or other obstruction. It the hole is inside a duct or is otherwise obstructed, measure the distance the hole must be moved and begin the process again from back inside the room where the computer is being placed.

■ If you can find the hole easily and it is clear of obstructions, enlarge the hole using a ⅜-inch drill bit. This should be large enough to accommodate your Ethernet cable and connector. If your connectors do not fit through the hole, use your drill to enlarge the hole to the appropriate size.

Figure 3.16

Place the guide wire so that it is visible above and below the floor.

If you cannot drill a hole that provides a clear path for your cable, we recommend that you seek the services of a professional electrician. An electrician is also the option you should use if you wish to install your network cable inside your walls and connect your cables directly into RJ-45 connectors fitted with a nice cover plate. We don't recommend trying an in-wall installation by yourself, unless you are experienced in these areas.

Laying Cable

While standing at the location for one of the computers, secure one end of the Ethernet cable to that position with masking tape or something heavy enough to hold it in place without crushing the cable. Securing the end of the cable in place is very important for when you begin stringing the Ethernet cable along its path leading from the location of one computer to the location of the next computer. Use a few plastic cable management clips (Figure 3.17) along the path to keep the cable secure while you continue installing it. However, we suggest that you use them sparingly until you find that the cable path and placement is what you want. When you are sure that the cable is long enough and fits through all of the drilled holes, you will then want to go back along the cable path and secure the cable using additional cable management clips.

Figure 3.17

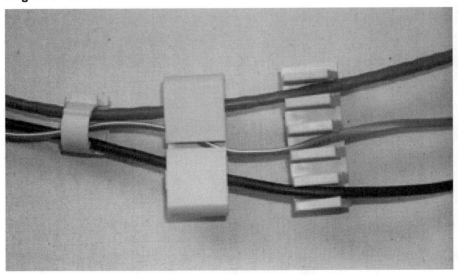

Use cable management clips to set the path of the cable.

NIC Card Installation

If you need to install a NIC in your computer, we suggest you follow the instructions included with your NIC. Just about every manufacturer provides installation and set-up instructions for installing their cards. If the NIC you are using does not have instructions or a product manual, you may want to get these items before you start, or if they are not available, get a NIC that has them. Following the specific installation instructions of the manufacturer may be a requirement of your warranty. Remember that you should always keep one hand on the computer case or wear an antistatic wrist guard when working on the inside of a computer. Figure 3.18 shows the NIC card being placed into an expansion slot.

If you plan on using a NIC card that you have removed from another computer or one that a friend has given you and you don't have the manufacturer's product manual or a device driver for the NIC, all is not lost. You may actually be able to use this card. First, check the card for a manufacturer's name and product number. If present, at least the manufacturer's name should be easy to find. Second, go to the manufacturer's Web site and see if you can find technical information for its NICs, looking to match a product, model, or serial number to the card you have. If you have no luck with this, there is another way to locate a device driver, without which the NIC is absolutely no good to you or your network.

Figure 3.18

A NIC card being installed in a computer.

Look on the NIC for a six-digit alphanumeric number (one that has letters and numbers mixed) in the pattern of 00A0C9 or the like. This number, called the organizationally unique identifer (OUI), which is pronounced "oh, you, eye" and not "wee," may be the first six digits of a much longer number that has a barcode line below it. Usually these numbers are found on stickers or labels placed near the top edge of the board. If the NIC has an OUI, you are in luck and can identify the manufacturer of the card easily, which also means you are almost assured of finding a device driver. The number 00A0C9 is an OUI assigned to the Intel Corporation.

The OUI number is assigned and administered by the Institute for Electrical and Electronic Engineers (IEEE), who keeps a database of who is assigned to which OUI. Rather than using the IEEE's Website (www.ieee.org) and searching for the manufacturer in their database, there is a very handy site you can use (www.windrivers.com/ identity/network) to look up the manufacturer of your NIC.

If your NIC has a number identified as "FCC ID:" you can also look up the manufacturer on the WinDrivers Web site using this number.

Please understand that you must have a device driver for your NIC to work in your computer. If you have a fairly new NIC card from a fairly well-known manufacturer, chances are good that Windows has a device driver for it in its files. But, if Windows draws a blank, you will need to find one to download, find the diskette or CD-ROM that came with the NIC, or buy a new NIC.

Be sure you read the instructions very carefully before you start installing the card. You may need to set some jumper plugs or toggle switches (called DIP switches) physically on the NIC before inserting it into the computer. If these actions are required, they will be spelled out on the manufacturer's instructions (another reason why you need them). Should you have questions during the installation, a very good place to find help is on the manufacturer's Web site, before you call their technical support line.

Some NICs come with a diskette or CD-ROM that provides a software set-up for the NIC. If this is the case, be sure to complete this process before proceeding to the next steps.

Windows Settings

You're almost there! By this point, you should be able to see your project shaping into a computer network. The cable is in place. You've installed your NIC cards. There are only a few steps left to complete your mission.

It is time to configure your Windows settings so that your computers will begin to look for each other and speak to each other. How you configure the Windows settings on your computers will be determined by whether you have Internet Sharing available on your network. Below are the steps you will need to take to configure the Windows settings for both Internet Sharing and Non-Internet Sharing networks.

Non-Internet Sharing Windows Settings
Complete the following steps for each computer on your network:

1. On the Windows desktop there is an icon called Network Neighborhood. Right-click (move the mouse pointer over the icon and click the right mouse button) on this icon (Figure 3.19).

2. Select the Properties option. The window shown in Figure 3.20 should be displayed.

3. Click on the Access Control tab and select the Share-level access control (Figure 3.21).

Figure 3.19

The Windows Desktop showing the Network Neighborhood icon.

Figure 3.20

The Network window.

Figure 3.21

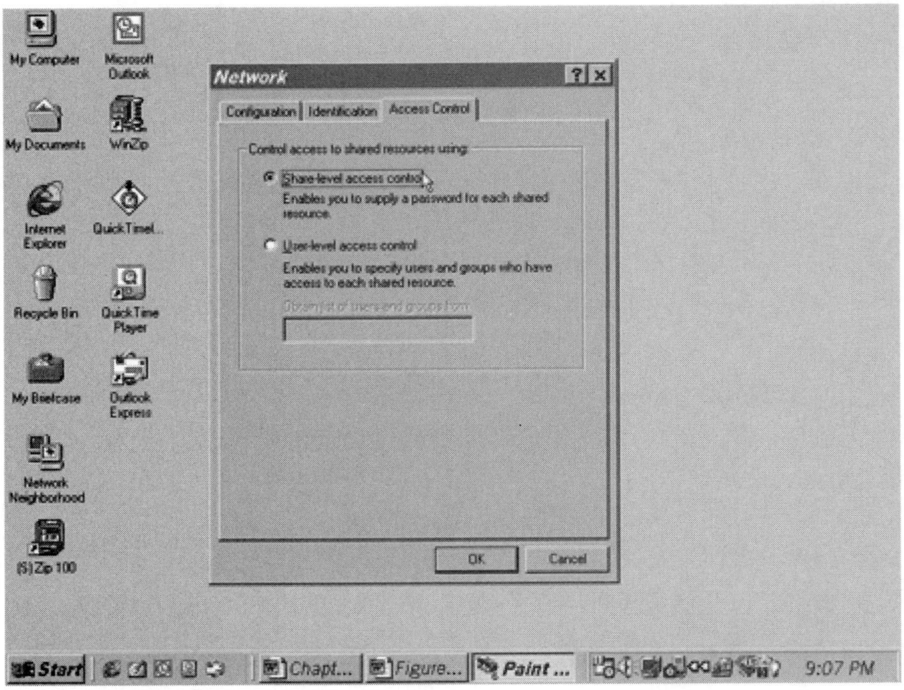

The Access Control tab.

4. Select the Identification tab, shown in Figure 3.22.

   a. In the text box next to the word Computer, type in a name for your computer. We advise that you give your computers names that will not be easily mistaken for one another, such as:

   Good:

   - Curly, Larry, and Moe

   - Samson and Delilah

   - Salt and Pepper

   Not Good:

   - Computer 1 and Computer 2 (avoid spaces and vague names)

   - Mike and Ike (too similar)

   - Larry, Daryl, and my other computer Darrel (avoid duplicates or sound-a-likes)

   b. In the text box next to the word Workgroup (Figure 3.23), type in a name for your computer network's group. You will use this same name on all computers, as it is the name

for your entire network. You can give them a name like
FUNGROUP or HOMEGROUP or just FUN or HOME.

Figure 3.22

The Identification tab.

   c. In the text box next to the word Computer Description, type
   in something that describes your computer. This will be a
   unique description that describes a specific computer. Our
   suggestion is to describe the computer according to its location or use, such as Mom's Computer, Dad's Computer,
   Kid's Computer, Office, Family Room, or Kitchen.

5. Click on the Configuration tab (Figure 3.23).

   a. Under the word Primary Network Logon, click on the small
   down arrow to the right of the list box and then select Client
   for Microsoft Networks.

   b. Under the words "The following network components are
   installed:" double-click on the words similar to "TCP/IP
   name of adapter" and then select the IP Address tab.

   c. Select the Specify an IP address radio button.

   d. Next to the words IP Address, type in an IP address similar
   to 192.168.0.X, where X is unique on each machine, and
   between the numbers 1 and 254.

Figure 3.23

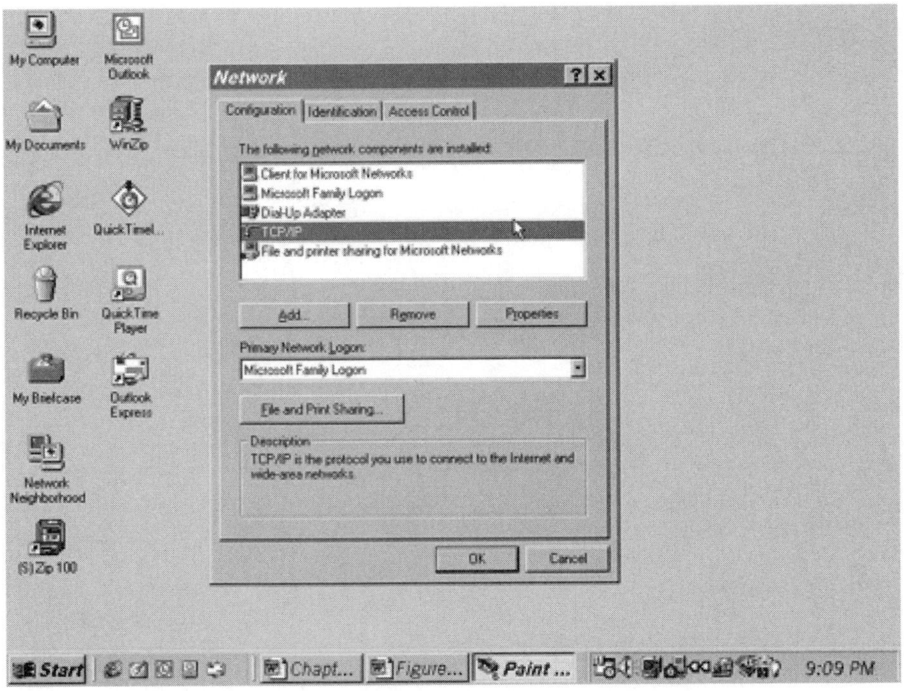

The Configuration tab.

e. Next to the words Subnet Mask, type in the numbers 255.255.255.0.

f. Select the WINS Configuration tab. Select the Disable DNS radio button.

g. You will not need to select the NetBIOS tab, Advanced tab, or the Bindings tab. We recommend that you do not change anything within these tabs.

Internet Sharing Windows Settings

Complete the following steps for each computer on your network.

1. Your proxy server will come with its own unique list of instructions for installation, which are dependent on the manufacturer. Please follow these instructions carefully. Contact your Internet service provider to verify any IP addresses or server names needed during the set-up.

2. At this point, you will need to have a 3½-inch floppy disk available along with your Windows 98 CD-ROM.

   a. On the Windows desktop, there is an icon titled My Computer. Double-click on this icon.

b. Double-click on the Control Panel icon. This displays the Control Panel window shown in Figure 3.24.

Figure 3.24

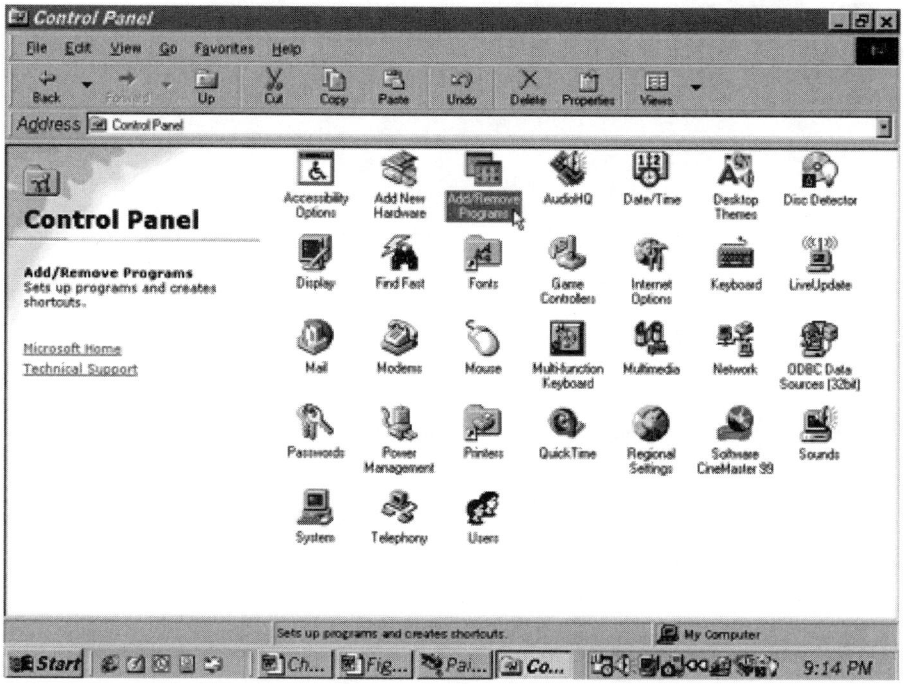

The Control Panel window.

c. Double-click on the Add/Remove Programs icon. The window is displayed in Figure 3.25.

d. Click on the Windows Setup tab. The window shown in Figure 3.26 appears. A small box may appear for a few seconds letting you know that Windows Setup is searching for installed components.

e. Double-click on the words Internet Tools.

f. Click the box next to the words Internet Connection Sharing. This will place a check mark in the box. If you have not installed and configured a NIC in your computer, a warning box will appear that tells you that the necessary hardware has not been installed. Until you have installed and configured the NIC, you will not be able to complete the selection of the Internet Connection Sharing option.

g. Click OK. You may be asked for your Windows 98 SE CD-ROM at this time; if so, insert the CD-ROM.

Figure 3.25

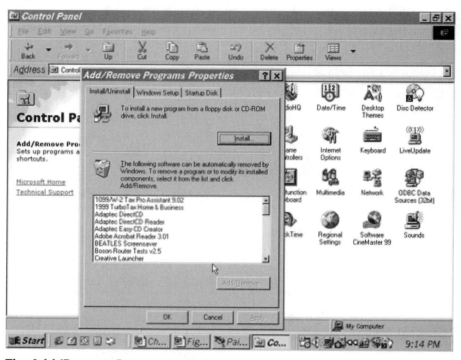

The Add/Remove Programs window.

Figure 3.26

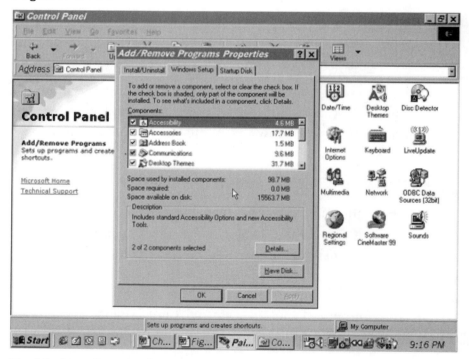

The Windows Setup tab.

When completed, the Internet Connection Sharing Wizard, shown in Figure 3.27, will open. It is advisable to trust the Wizards when you are not sure of an option.

   i. Click the Next button.

   ii. Select the connection method.

   iii. Click the Next button.

   iv. Insert the floppy disk and click the Next button.

h. Click Yes to restart your computer.

Figure 3.27

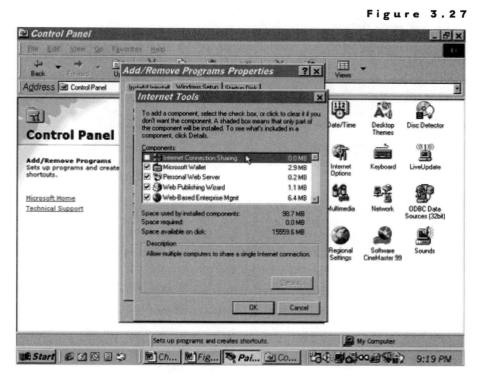

The Internet Connection Wizard.

3. You may use the floppy disk that you just created to set up each computer in your network instantly rather than to go through all of the steps listed in step 2. To do this:

a. Insert the floppy disk into another computer on your network.

b. Click on the Start button.

c. Select Run.

d. Type in a:\icsclset.exe and click on Enter, as shown in Figure 3.28.

Figure 3.28

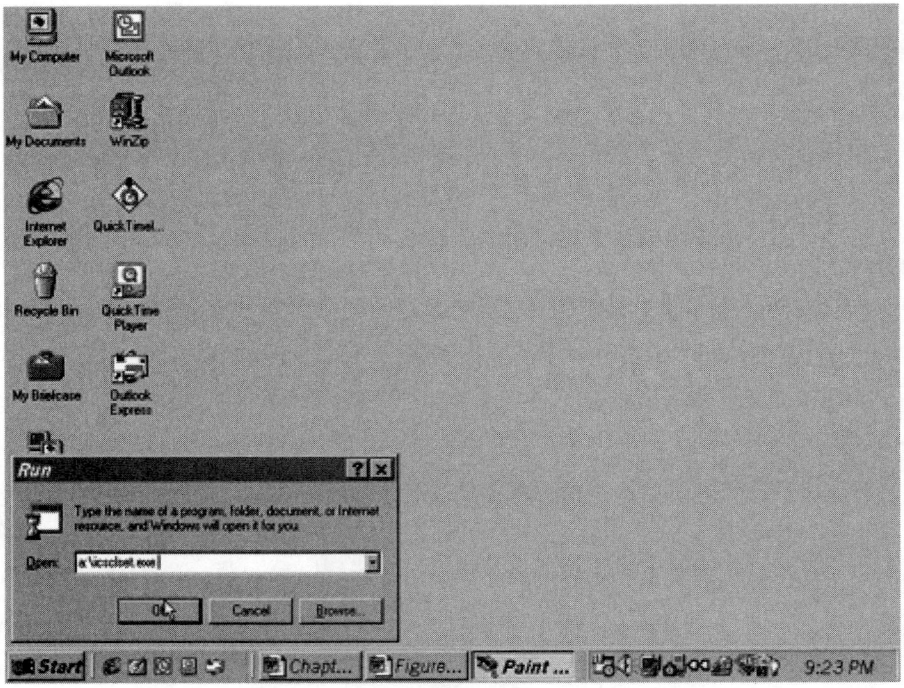

The Start Run box.

    e. Click on the OK button.

Cable Connection

If you have two computers for your network, no more and certainly no less, you may now connect them with the Ethernet cable. If you have more than two computers and are using a hub, you will want to connect one end of each cable to the hub and the other end of those cables to the NIC in each computer.

The cable connects to the NIC as shown in Figure 3.29. Well, what do you know? It's beginning to look a lot like a network.

Connecting with a DSL Service

If your network is to be connected to the Internet through a digital subscriber line (DSL) connection, there isn't a lot of difference to the set-up than that to connect to a network hub. Your customer premise equipment (CPE) is one of three possible types of equipment. The most commonly used CPE is a DSL modem and the next most common device is a DSL bridge. Both of these devices operate on layer 2 of the OSI model (see Chapter 1), which means they interconnect using physical addresses (MAC addressing).

Figure 3.29

Connecting the network cable to the NIC.

Your service provider should let you know whether you are using dynamic host configuration protocol (DHCP) or have been assigned a static IP address. If you have been assigned a static IP, your service provider should help you through the configuration of your host computer to assign it the assigned IP address.

If your service provider has supplied you with a router (which indicates right off that you are probably using synchronous DSL or SDSL, then you should talk to your DSL provider to provide your router with its IP addresses and the set-up of network address translation (NAT), firewall services, and any other services available on the router.

Don't Underestimate the Need and Value of a Firewall

If you are using DSL services, and even if you are using dial-up connections, you should investigate the use of a firewall on your system. If you are using DSL, you don't have much choice. Your network is effectively online around the clock, 24 hours a day, 7 day a week, sitting open to the world with a static IP address. That's about as much of a sitting duck as an Internet workstation can be.

Two types of firewall are available: hardware and software. A hardware firewall is a stand-alone device that plugs into your network and, after being configured into your network, filters all incoming (and outgoing, if you desire) access for services. If a source or unknown address tries to enter your network, it is denied access. People you trust are allowed to pass through the firewall to access resources on your service. Software firewalls essentially perform the same activities on your networked computer. Software firewalls are generally easier to set-up and configure and are usually installed must faster than a hardware device (which may also require its own IP address). One good site for a software firewall (that was free last time we checked) is www.zonealarm.com.

Either way, hardware or software, protect your system, DSL or not, with a firewall. Not everyone on the Internet can be trusted.

Power

We suggest that you always use a surge protector when plugging any of your network equipment into an AC power outlet. A surge protector, like the one shown in Figure 3.30, can save you from irreparable damage should you have a power fluctuation in your electrical lines. It doesn't take much of an electrical current spike to damage a computer, printer, or other network device.

Figure 3.30

A surge suppressing plug strip.

Plug your computers into surge protector strips, one strip per computer. Then plug in your hub and/or proxy servers into their surge protector strip. Okay, plug in the strips to their respected AC outlet. They're alive!

Windows Share Settings

If you plan on sharing a device across your network such as a CD-ROM, hard drive, printer, or modem, you will need to change the Windows settings to reflect that they will be shared devices. The following examples will show you the steps that are required to allow the sharing of device.

File and Printer Sharing

1. Double-click on the Network Neighborhood icon to open the Network dialog box, shown in Figure 3.31.

Figure 3.31

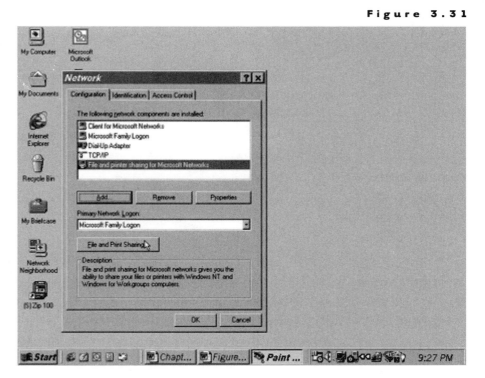

Network Properties window.

2. Click on File and Print Sharing. The window shown in Figure 3.32 is displayed.

Figure 3.32

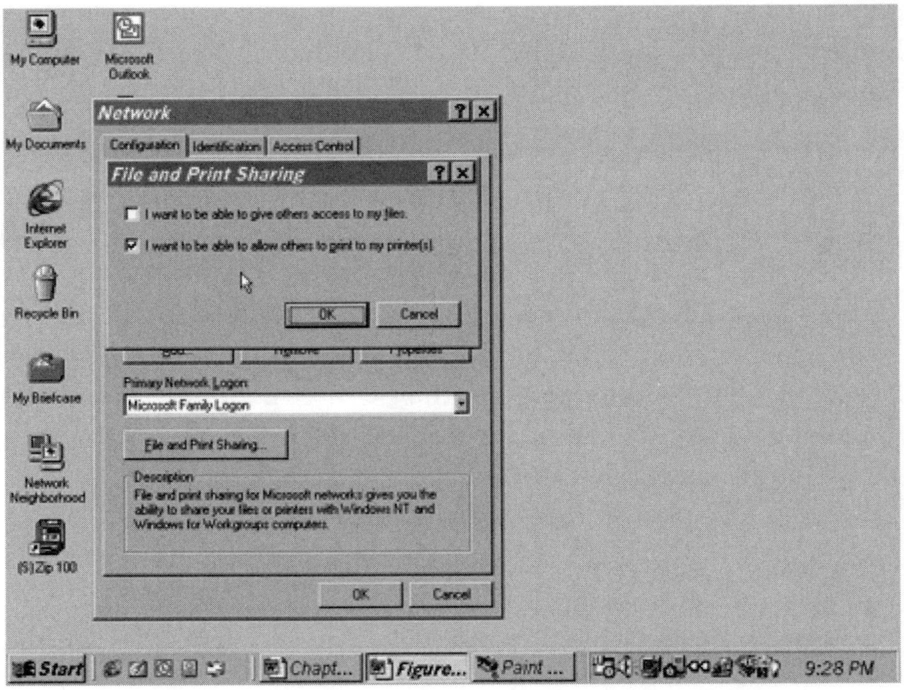

File and Print Sharing options window.

3. Select the check box for the sharing options you want. A check mark indicates the feature is activated.

4. Click OK.

You can also open the Network dialog box by clicking on Start at the bottom left-hand corner of your desktop, clicking on Settings, clicking on Control Panel, and then double-clicking on Network. Remember, you can only share a printer that is connected to your computer.

Sharing Your Printer
1. Click Start, select Settings, and then click on Printers. The Printers windows, shown in Figure 3.33, is displayed.

2. Click on the printer name that you want to share.

3. Click on File at the top of your window; click on Properties

4. Click once on the Sharing tab, to display the window shown in Figure 3.34, then click Shared As.

Figure 3.33

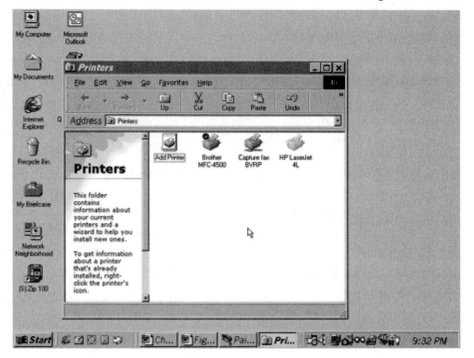

Printers Window.

Figure 3.34

Printer Sharing tab.

Testing Your Network

You have arrived at the second to last step in building your own home network, testing. If you have opted to share files across your network, you should attempt to open those files from a remote computer on your network. For example, if you are sharing files on Computer A (Larry), then you will want to attempt to access those files through Computer B (Moe).

You will also want to attempt to print from all computers on your network. A network can be looked upon as a puzzle. If pieces are missing, then the network is incomplete. It will not function properly. If you find that printing or file sharing will not operate correctly, go back through the steps outlined above to see if you could have possibly missed a step, or piece of the puzzle.

If you find that all of the pieces to your network puzzle fit together and your operations are running smoothly, it is time to go to the next and final step.

Gloating

You may now take pride in your accomplishment. You have just *built your own home network*. You may now call all of your friends, family, and co-workers and brag about your newfound skill. Congratulations on behalf of the authors of *How to Build Your Own Home Network*. We're proud of you!

10BaseT

A cable or device that supports a 10-Mbps baseband twisted-pair network.

10Base2

The designation used for thin coaxial cable.

10Base5

The designation used for thick coaxial cable.

100BaseF

Designates a fiber optic network with 100 Mbps of bandwidth.

100BaseT

The designation used for a 100 Mbps baseband twisted-pair network.

Active hub

A hub that acts like a repeater to amplify the signal being passed on to the devices connected to it.

Application layer

Layer 7 of the OSI model; it provides for user authentication, privacy, and constraints on data.

ARCNet

A network technology that is implemented on the star topology.

Attenuation

The point at which the signal sent through a cable begins to fade and becomes unusable.

Bandwidth

The capacity in bits per second of a cable medium.

Baseband

A network transmission mode that uses one channel to send digital data over a line.

BNC connector

A connector used for thin and thick coaxial cable.

BNC connector

Broadband

A network transmission mode that uses analog signaling to send data over a wide range of frequencies.

Bus topology

Network nodes are connected through connectivity devices, such as a hub, to a central cable, called a backbone, that runs the length of the network. Commonly used for Ethernet.

Category 3 (Cat 3) wire

A four-pair network cable that supports bandwidth up to 10 Mbps and is the minimum standard for 10BaseT networks.

Category 4 (Cat 4) wire

A four-pair network cable that is commonly used in 16-Mbps token ring networks.

Category 5 (Cat 5) wire

A four-pair network cable that supports bandwidths up to 100 Mbps.

Client

A network workstation that requests and receives services from a network server. Network clients request services of the network server.

Client/server

The network type that includes a server and clients. Permission to access the resources of the network is managed by a central network administrator.

Coaxial cable

A type of network cable very much like that used to connect your television set to the cable box and the VCR. There are two types of coaxial cable used in networks, a thick wire and a thin wire.

Coaxial cable

Connection-less

A communications mode that requires none of the handshaking and monitoring of the connection-oriented communications mode.

Connection-oriented

The type of connection that requires a connection be established and requires that acknowledgments be sent to verify data was received before sending more.

Crimper

A special tool used to attach RJ-11 and RJ-45 connectors to the end of a UTP cable.

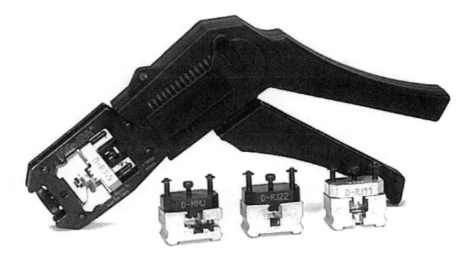

Crimper

Datagram

A small, variable length bundle of data that is sent over a network.

Data Link layer

Layer 2 of the OSI model; it supports the physical layer (layer 1) by providing physical device addressing, error-control, and timing.

EISA (extended ISA)

A 32-bit architecture developed to enhance the ISA structure.

EMI (electromagnetic interference)

Electronic interference that is generated from network cables, light fixtures, and other types of electrical devices.

Ethernet

A shared network technology, on which all network workstations share the available bandwidth, which can range from 10 Mbps to 1 Gbps. Ethernet is the most commonly used access method for home networks.

Fiber optic

This type of network cable uses thin strands of glass to carry digital data that has been transformed into light impulses. It is very expensive, hard to work with, and certainly not worth the effort for a home network.

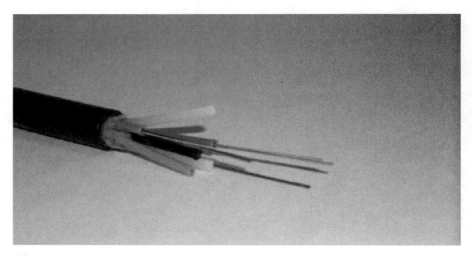

Fiber optic

Gateway

A combination of hardware and software that is used to connect two networks with different network protocols and allow them to communicate with one another.

Hub

A network device used to connect one or more workstations to a network.

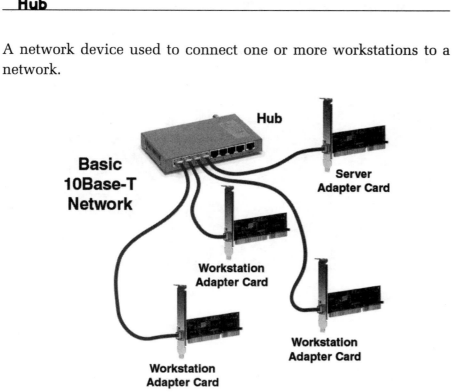

Hub

Internet

Most commonly referred to as "the Internet;" it is the global interconnection of millions of networks and computers to form a global-wide area network.

IP (Internet Protocol) address

The network or logical address of a node. It is made up of four eight-bit numbers (each called an *octet*) that combine to identify not only the workstation or node but also its network. The IP address identifies a workstation to the LAN, the WAN, and beyond.

IRQ (interrupt request)

An internal device used by the computer to communicate with its peripherals.

ISA (industry standard architecture)

An older 16-bit bus architecture that is still very commonly used.

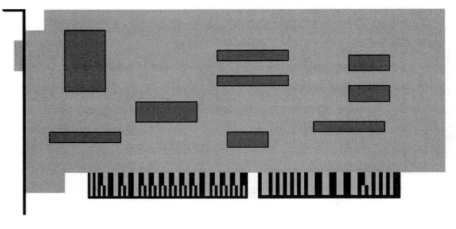

ISA

LAN (local area network)

A network that consists of two or more nodes, usually in a relatively small (local) area. The workstations of a LAN are connected for the primary purpose of sharing local data and resources. A home network is typically a LAN, as is the network in a small office, or the one in a manufacturing plant.

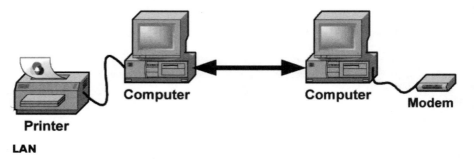

LAN

MAC (media access control) address

The physical address of a node. The unique MAC address is permanently, electronically "burned" into network adapters, including NICs, by their manufacturer. The MAC address is used to uniquely identify each node attached to the network.

Media

The plural form of the word *medium*, which refers to the material at the core of a network cable. On a UTP cable, copper is the cable medium. All of the cables on a network form the cable media.

NetBIOS (network basic input/output system)

A standard network protocol that is used to support other network protocols by creating a connection, passing messages, and handling error detection and recovery.

NetBEUI (NetBIOS extended user interface)

A standard message transport option to NetBIOS that is used for communicating within a single LAN.

Network

Two or more computers or peripheral devices, such as printers, CD-ROM towers, scanners, and the like, that are directly connected for the purpose of sharing the hardware, software, and data resources of the connected devices.

Network adapter

A hardware device, which is inserted into a networked workstation and allows it to communicate with other networked elements. The network adapter receives and translates incoming signals from the network for the workstation and translates and sends outgoing communications to the network.

Network layer

Layer 3 of the OSI model; it defines how data is routed to a destination address.

NIC (network interface card)

The most common type of network adapter, which is generally installed inside the computer's case in an expansion slot located on the computer's main board. A NIC is by far the most common form of network adapter used to connect home and office computers to a network.

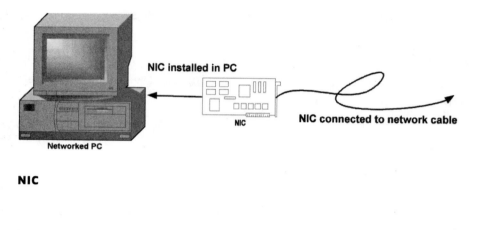

NIC

Node

A networked workstation or any other device that has been attached to the network. A node, a term derived from the word *nodule*, is actually the reference point used by the network to identify anything attached to the network.

Operating system

The system software that manages the hardware, provides a user interface, and controls data storage on a computer.

OSI model

Officially the open system interconnection reference model, a standard that defines the various functions, defined as layers, that a network packet passes through in moving from its source to its destination. The seven-layered OSI model applies to local networks and to large networks, including the Internet.

| Application Layer |
| Presentation Layer |
| Session Layer |
| Transport Layer |
| Network Layer |
| Data Link Layer |
| Physical Layer |

OSI model

Packet

A small, variable length data bundle that is usually 256 to 2000 bytes long.

Passive hub

A network device that passes a signal to the devices connected to it without amplifying the signal.

PCI (peripheral component interface)

A 32-bit bus architecture that is a local bus architecture, which means that it shares a pathway between the CPU, memory, and peripheral devices on the computer motherboard.

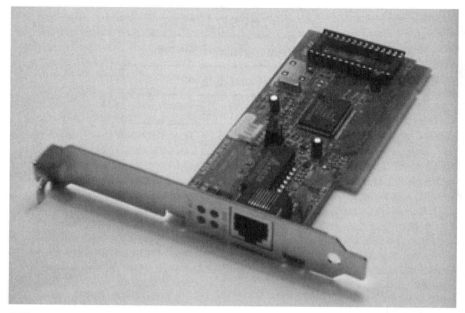

PCI

PCMCIA (Personal Computer Memory Card Industry Association)

Also called the PC card bus; it is used on notebook and other portable computers.

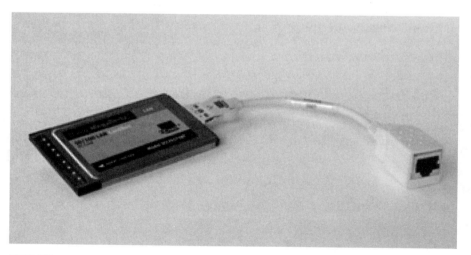

PCMCIA

Peer

Another name for a workstation or a node directly connected to another computer, which means that it is an equal participant in a network.

Peer-to-peer network

A network owned and operated cooperatively by the owners (users) of the networked workstations. Each individual user decides independently of other network users who has and does not have access to his or her computer and its resources. Most home networks are peer-to-peer networks.

Physical layer

Layer 1 of the OSI model. This layer defines how the electrical bit stream is carried over the hardware and mechanical devices of the network.

Plug-and-Play

Often abbreviated as PnP, plug-and-play devices require little or no configuration or set up because they are automatically assigned any system resources they need and are enabled for use when detected by the computer.

Presentation layer

Layer 6 of the OSI model; it manages the conversion of incoming and outgoing data from one data format to another.

Protocol

The rules of communication under which networks operate. A protocol prescribes how the requests, messages, and other signals are formatted and transmitted over the network.

Repeater

A hardware device that regenerates any signal it receives and sends it on.

Ring topology

The network backbone is installed as a loop, or ring, and the workstations are attached to the primary cable at various points on the ring.

RJ-11

The standard telephone line connector that connects four wires.

RJ-11

RJ-45

The standard UTP connector that connects eight wires.

RJ-45

Routing

The process used to determine the best path and to forward data along that path from a source network or network segment to a destination network address.

Router

A network device that directs, or routes, packets across networks. A router works with a message's IP address to determine the best path to its destination.

Server

A networked computer that provides support, in the form of data or other services, requested from the networked clients.

Session layer

Layer 5 of the OSI model; it sets up and terminates conversations, exchanges, and dialogs between applications over the network.

Sneaker-net

A computer or set of computers that share data only by a person physically carrying a diskette or other storage medium from one machine to the next.

Stand-alone computer

A computer that is not connected to other computers and, as a result, cannot share resources except over a sneaker-net.

Star topology

Network nodes are connected directly to a clustering network device, such as a hub or server, creating a starlike pattern.

STP (shielded twisted-pair)

A type of network cabling in which the twisted pairs of copper wire are shielded with a metal sheath that absorbs EMI. STP is more expensive and is usually unnecessary for most home networks.

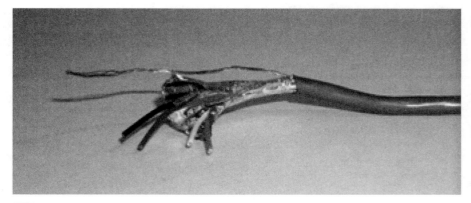

STP

TCP/IP (transmission control protocol/Internet protocol)

Probably the most common protocol in use on networks today. TCP/IP is actually a suite of protocols, each of which sets the rules and standards for a specific network action.

Token ring

This network technology is implemented on the ring topology.

Topology

The physical arrangement of the network. Bus, ring, and star are the most common topologies found on networks.

Transceiver

The device on the network adapter that transmits and receives data to and from the network.

Transport layer

Layer 4 of the OSI model; it provides end-to-end control for transferring data over the network.

UTP (unshielded twisted pair)

A networking cable made up of two strands of insulated copper wires that are twisted around each other inside a light, unshielded plastic sheath. This type of cable is easily found and generally inexpensive.

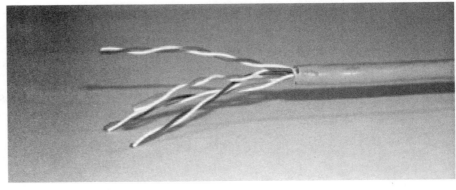

UTP

USB (universal serial bus)

A plug-and-play interface that allows devices to be added to the computer without an adapter card and while it is running.

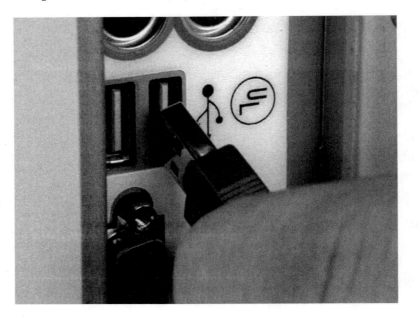

USB

Vampire tap

A connector type used on thick coaxial cable, which clamps into and pierces the cable to make its connection.

WAN (wide area network)

A network that interconnects two or more LANs using some form of telecommunications lines, such as telephone or dedicated, leased high-speed lines.

Workstation

A computer that has been attached to a network. Workstation is just another way to say "networked computer."

index

Note: Boldface numbers indicate illustrations.

100BaseF, 30, 89
100BaseT, 30, 89
10Base2, 30, 89
10Base5, 30, 89
10BaseT, 20, 30, 35, 89

A

Access Control, Windows configuration, 74, **75**
Active hubs, 21, 90
Adapter unit interface (AUI), 26
Adapters (*See* network adapters)
Add/Remove Programs, Windows configuration, 79, **80**
Addressing, 17–18
AnyPoint network adapter, 38, **39**
AnyPort Phoneline network adapter, 47, **47**
Application layer, OSI, 16, 90
ARCNet networks, 20–21, 90
Attenuation, 21, 90

B

Backbones, 18
Bandwidth, 29–30, 44, 90
Baseband networks, 29, 90
Bayonet connectors, 48
BNC connectors, 48, **48**, 90, **91**
Broadband networks, 29, 91
Bus architecture, 25, 65, 66
Bus architecture, 23–24, **24**, 36, **37**
Bus topologies, 8, **9**, 18, 91

C

Cables (*See* wires and cabling)
Caching, 58
Categories (CAT) of cabling, 45–46, 91, 92
Category 3 cabling, 45–46, 91
Category 4 cabling, 45–46, 91
Category 5 cabling, 45–46, 92
CD-ROMs, Share settings, Windows, 85–87, **85, 86, 87**
Classification of networks, 8–10
Client/server networks, 10–11, **11**, 54, 92
Clients, 10, 92
Clips to hold wires in place , 62, **62**, 67, **68**, 71, **72**
Coaxial cables, 6, **6**, 30, 43, 92, **92**
    bayonet connectors, 48
    BNC connectors, 48, **48**
Computer networks defined, 2–3, **3**
Computer placement, 54, 59–69
Configuration tab, Windows configura-

tion, 77, **78**
Configuring your network with
    Windows, 74–82, **75–82**
    Access Control, 74, **75**
    Add/Remove Programs, 79, **80**
    Configuration tab, 77, **78**
    Control Panel settings, 79–81, **79, 80**
    File and Print Sharing, 85–87, **86, 87**
    Identification setting, 76–77, **77**
    Internet Connection Sharing Wizard, 81
    Internet sharing settings, 78–82, **79–82**
    Internet Tools, 79, **81**
    IP address, 77–78
    Network Neighborhood, 74, **75**, 85, **85**
    non-Internet sharing settings, 74–78, **75–78**
    Properties, 74, **75**
    proxy server, 78
    Share settings, 85–87, **85, 86, 87**
Connection types, 13–15
Connection-less sessions, 13, **14**, 92
Connection-oriented sessions, 13, **14**, 93
Connectivity devices, 21–22
Connectors, 34
    bayonet connectors, 48
    BNC connectors , 48, **48**, 90, **91**
    crimper tool, 50, **51**, 93, **93**
    purchasing, 66
    RJ-11 connectors, 47, **47**, 102, **102**
    RJ-45 connectors, 46, **47**, 66, **68**, 102, **103**
    T-connectors, 48, **49**
    terminators, 48, **49**
    vampire taps, 48–49, **50**, 106
Connectors for NICs, 28
Connectors for UTP, 46–49, **47, 48, 49**
Control Panel settings, Windows configuration, 79–81, **79, 80**
Costs, 49
Crimper tool, 50, **51**, 93, **93**

D

Data buses, 23
Data Link layer, OSI, 15, 93
Datagrams, 13, 15, 93
Digital subscriber line (DSL) connections, 82–84
DIP switch settings for NIC, 40, 74
Domain name system (DNS), 18